The GEM of EDENVALE

THE HISTORIC HAYES MANSION OF SAN JOSE, CALIFORNIA

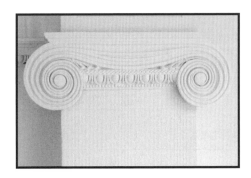

The GEM of EDENVALE

THE HISTORIC HAYES MANSION OF SAN JOSE, CALIFORNIA

Nancy L. Newlin

Nancy L. Newlin

Renasci

San Jose, California

Published by:
Renasci
P.O. Box 28338
San Jose, California 95159-8338

Printed in the United States of America.

ISBN: 0-9641102-0-2

Dedicated to former San Jose City Council member Judy Stabile, the San Jose City Council, and the citizens of San Jose who preceded me in their appreciation of the Hayes mansion and who assured its preservation for generations to come.

Book design: Nancy Newlin
Cover design: Stephen Connor
Cover photographs: Nancy Newlin
Front cover: The Hayes Renaissance Conference Center
Back cover: Wall covering; terra cotta detail.
Illustrations: Nancy Newlin, Dave Olmos
Editing: Kathi Vian
Production: Catherine Lush
Coordination: Stephen Connor

Research funds were provided in part by grants from the Sourisseau Academy Foundation, Department of History, San Jose State University.

Contents

We need to tell the real stories of the lives of the people who built these places. The stories of what possessed them to build the way they did, where they got their design ideas, where, for that matter, they got the money to build them. And all of the other authentic tales of the interrelationships between the places and the folks who lived there. We need to explain through these stories why we are right to preserve these places. And we also want to tell the often incredible, often exasperating, but ultimately engrossing stories of how they were preserved and who preserved them.

J. Jackson Walter
former President, National Trust for Historic Preservation

Introduction
The Road to Edenvale

A short drive south of downtown San Jose, California, brings you to a large building on Edenvale Avenue, a building that seems conspicuously out of place. It's huge. Part of it looks new and part of it looks old. The signs welcome you to the "Hayes Renaissance Conference Center." You can't help but wonder: "How did this building come to be here?"

Imagine, for a moment or two, a 51-year-old man and a 77-year-old woman, each of them with a particular gift of vision, speaking together at the turn of the century. The man's vision is architectural. The woman's is spiritual. You imagine them working together, envisioning a house, a suitable home for the woman's unusual family, a structure that will not be as vulnerable to fire as the previous house that stood on this site. You might also imagine that it took the vision of many others to preserve the spirit of this house in its present incarnation as a conference center. And you would be right.

The Hayes mansion, reincarnated in 1994 as the Hayes Renaissance Conference Center, almost didn't make it to 1994. Built in 1905 to replace a splendid Queen Anne Victorian on the same site, it was originally the residence for the Hayes family. The family matriarch, Mary Hayes Chynoweth, was not only the guiding force in her family's evolution from poor farm origins to considerable wealth, but was also a healer and spiritual guide to the community. However, she never saw this house finished, and after her death, and the deaths of her two sons, the family sold it in 1954.

The years from 1954 until the opening of the conference center in 1994 were not easy for the house. It changed hands many times. Some of its owners stripped it of its hardware. Later, vandals broke into it. A series of arson fires also damaged some of its fine interior woodwork. Through the years, its new neighbors, living in houses that began to surround it, drove by regularly or looked over their fences at it. They wondered what would become of the stately structure as the grounds were taken over by weeds and the once magnificent 40-acre family park to the north became the Frontier Village amusement park.

What happened was a miracle of preservation. The mansion's downward trend intersected fortuitously with the upward national movement to save, protect, and, if at all possible, restore historic properties. Thus, to see it today, pristine and elegant, is to see the story of many people: its original owners, the Hayes family; its architect, George Page; and hundreds of people who, over the years, have taken an interest and, in some small measure, have seen to it that the mansion survived.

That is the story of this book. It begins, in Chapter 1, with the matriarch of the Hayes family, who first had visions of the Edenvale site while still living in a mining town in Wisconsin. Chapter 2 sketches the life of George Page, a prodigious, turn-of-the-century architect who deserves to be better known. Chapters 3 through 5 provide a close-up look at the two Hayes mansions and the estate as a whole—as well as the details of daily life on the estate. Finally, Chapter 6 tells the story of how many people rallied around the house, determined not to let it fall victim to the fate of countless other historic buildings around the country. Through their efforts, the Hayes Renaissance Conference Center exists today, the realization of a vision that will catapult the mansion into the next century, assure its future, and bring Edenvale to prominence once more.

Chapter 1

Mary Hayes Chynoweth
Wealth Through Spiritual Guidance, For Community Service

Mrs. Chynoweth was of a profound religious temperament and preached the doctrine of good, pure living, both for the salvation of the soul and the betterment of the body. She was believed by many to possess extraordinary powers of healing, and during the eighteen years of her sojourn in California is credited with having restored numerous petitioners to health. She made no pretense to spiritualistic power, yet inculcated the theory that pure, optimistic thinking and rational diet were the basis of sound health. To this treatment she was wont to add manual application—laying on of hands— in some manner like massage. She was truly saintly in that she took no pay either for preaching or helping the sick. It is said that, through instinct or revelation, she indicated the exact spot near Hurley into which her sons dug and found the iron which brought them riches.

—*The Madison [Wisconsin] Democrat*, August 1, 1906

Mary Hayes Chynoweth, 1825 to 1905

The story of Edenvale begins not in California, but in the small New York town of Holland, in the year 1825. There, Mary Folsom was born, the ninth child of Abraham and Miriam Folsom. Three of the Folsom's earlier children had already died. But this one would survive and grow up to become an extraordinary woman—a woman of special gifts and a passion for giving.

A childhood in small-town New York

Abraham Folsom was a Free Will Baptist minister, as were most of his siblings. He didn't charge for his ministerial services, choosing instead to support his family by working as a blacksmith. Miriam Folsom, in feeble health from multiple childbirths, could barely do household chores.

By the time Mary was four, her father had moved the family to a farm in the town of Cuba, New York. There, Mary took on responsibilities and physical work far beyond her years. She cared for her younger sister, and she learned to sew, weave, and spin. She was precocious, too, surprising everyone by helping her older sister set up a loom without any instruction. Whatever her tasks, Mary did them with cheerfulness and competence.

At 12, Mary took work outside the home, washing, ironing, milking, spinning, and cheesemaking for a household of seven.[1] Her wages helped support her own family, and her experience developed in her a spirit of hard work and generosity—a spirit that she later passed on to her sons and grandchildren. Many of them would eventually work on the Edenvale estate as children, making the same wages as the farm workers and using their earnings for gifts and charity.[2]

Life was not all work for the young Mary, however. The Folsom household bustled with religious inquiry, as local religious folk and clergymen came to talk with Mary's father. Mary listened and sometimes participated with far more understanding and sensitivity than one would normally expect of a child. Abraham welcomed Mary in these talks, and through them, a strong and loving bond was forged between father and daughter.

Mary's older brother William also appreciated her intelligence and capability. When she turned 15, he decided that she could earn more money and use her talents to better advantage. He persuaded the Clarksville, New York, schoolboard to hire her as a teacher. As a prerequisite, though, Mary had to pass an oral exam. Mary herself was doubtful. She had attended no more than a year of school in her life—going to school made her sick and nauseous.[3] But from an early age, she had read extensively, immersing herself in books every chance she got. She also learned from her brothers, watching them perform mathematical calculations and borrowing their schoolbooks. When she took the schoolboard's exam, she passed easily and began her teaching career. This work occupied her until she was 22, when the family again needed her at home.

Reuniting the family in Wisconsin

As Mary was growing to adulthood, several of the Folsom children had married and moved west to Wisconsin. In 1849, when Mary was 24, Abraham decided it was time to reunite his family—and to explore the opportunities in the new territory. So he bought a farm three miles from Waterloo, Wisconsin, and moved the family there.

Mary and her older sister, Lucina, stayed behind at first, managing the New York farm until it sold the following year. Then they joined the family in Wisconsin. Once there, Mary again took up teaching, earning quite a reputation:

The school was at Waterloo, and in it were several unruly boys who had turned out two preceding teachers. They were waiting to try the same trick on the teacher from the East, whose reputation had preceded her. Entering the schoolroom she spoke a few words of greeting; [the words] were not much in themselves, but threw out a magnetic touch that went to the hearts of these boys, who, from that day, became her most devoted and faithful pupils.[4]

The move to Waterloo was not without its costs, however. Because the house in Cuba had sold for less than the price of the new farm, Mary's earnings were not her own: her salary was needed to meet the family's mortgage payments.

The Power comes to Mary Folsom

As Mary was establishing herself as a teacher in Wisconsin, spiritualism was gaining popularity across the American continent. Spiritualists were people who believed they could speak with the dead. The dead, in turn, communicated through the spiritualists by causing them to rap on a table or speak in strange tongues. For example, the Fox sisters, who were also from New York, were famous for table rappings.[5] This phenomenon interested Mary's father, who sought to determine if it was indeed possible to communicate with the dead. Two of Mary's sisters were also intrigued, but Mary herself was not. The fascination with spiritualism disturbed both Mary and her mother, who felt it was the antithesis of the religion they practiced.[6]

However, everything changed for Mary one day when she was 27. She suddenly told her students that she would not be returning as their teacher. At the time, she didn't understand what made her say such a thing, but rather she simply had an inner feeling that she should resign from teaching. Then, the following Sunday, Mary's sisters went off to a meeting to hear Cora L. V. Scott, a spiritualist who had been one of Mary's

students. While they were gone, Mary had an experience that changed her life forever. In her own words, as told to a friend many years later, this is what happened:

Everything was done by eleven o'clock, and after washing my hands, I was crossing the kitchen with a basin of water, when, suddenly, some unknown Force pressed me down upon my knees, helpless. Of my own will I could not move nor see nor speak; but a compelling Power moved my tongue to prayer in language or languages unknown to me or to my father. The gentleman boarding with us said he recognized words of both German and French. No, I never studied and did not know any foreign language. "How do I account for it?" I do not know, unless it was the prophecy of what happened afterwards, when I spoke to Germans, French and Poles in their native tongues, and they understood me perfectly. O, yes, hundreds of people have heard it.—But as I was saying, the Power lifted me from my knees, took my father's Bible, and turned to a page down which it pointed my finger, read aloud the selection which states what the apostles were appointed to do; to preach, to heal, to cast out devils, to speak in tongues. Father recognized that my body was subject to a great power.[7]

Friends, neighbors, and other members of the church soon heard of her experience, as word of it spread rapidly through the small community of Waterloo. The following day, a local man who had sustained a severe cut asked to have Mary attend to him as a test of her new powers. She placed her hands on the cut, curing it and saving the man's finger. Thus began her lifelong mission to heal the sick of mind and body and follow the direction the Power gave her.

Her first decision was to begin a year of fasting on bread and water, going from town to town in southern Wisconsin, tending to the sick. Sometimes the Power directed her to go places or call on people without any clear notion of why she was needed—until she arrived and inevitably found someone who was ailing. Sometimes her diagnosis ran counter to that of the presiding physician, but her prescriptions of simple tonics, made from natural ingredients such as tree bark and herbs, often cured the problem. In addition to tonics, she would sometimes lay her hands on a patient, easing the pain or fever and, at the same time, determining the exact affliction. Often, she took on the symptoms of the disease herself for a short time until both she and the patient were cured. If a patient failed to follow her instructions, however, Mary herself would be relieved of the disease, and the patient's cure would cease.

Mary also developed a philosophy about correct diet, ". . . consisting chiefly of grains, fruits and vegetables, very little meat and no pork, tea, coffee, or alcohol. It was given to her that this would conserve human force and nourish mental and spiritual growth by cooling the blood and rendering the temperament more equable—a sure way to lessen disease."[8] Using this variety of techniques, Mary healed people suffering from cancer, tuberculosis, pneumonia, and many other serious diseases, as well as cuts and broken bones.[9]

While Mary felt a strong desire to pursue this new direction that the Power had set out for her—and not to ask for money for her services—she was greatly concerned about the effects of her choice on her family's financial security. Her father urged her to follow the Power anyway, trusting that they would be provided for in some way. His trust proved well founded, and in the end, Mary's work brought the necessary support for the family. Some people offered her money, which she sent to her family, while others offered a place for her to stay or sent her clothing and other necessities. Some even sent money directly to Mary's parents to help with their mortgage.

Mary begins her family

By late 1853, Mary's brothers had all married and moved away from home. Mary was away on her healing missions most of the time and had no steady income. Her parents were now in the later years of their lives, and with only Lucina at home, they could no longer manage the farm by themselves. Fortunately, a neighbor offered a solution.

Anson E. Hayes, a widower with a five-year-old daughter, had recently moved to Wisconsin from New York, where he had worked as a construction engineer on the Erie Canal. When he purchased a farm between the towns of Waterloo and Portland, he decided that he needed help with his household. He invited the Folsoms to move into his house, suggesting that Mrs. Folsom and Mary's younger sister, Lucina, could keep house and take care of his daughter, May. After consulting with Mary, the Folsoms turned over their farm to one of their sons and accepted Anson Hayes's proposal.

Anson Hayes had not yet met Mary, but he had heard of her work and admired her for it. During the brief visits she made to her parents, Anson and Mary came to know each other, and before long, Anson asked her to marry him. He assured her that he would assist here in her work in any way he could. For her part, Mary found that they got along well together and were in agreement about their life's work. Rather than seeing marriage as a hindrance to her mission, she saw it—and the children who would surely come with it—as part of her destiny. The two were married in May of 1854, when Mary was 28 and Anson was 41.

Over the years, Mary and Anson had three sons: Everis Anson (1855), Jay Orley (1857), and Charles Carroll (1861). Of the three sons, Carroll seemed to be the one who was blessed with the gift of healing. As Mary said, "My child-power for soothing pain was in his little hands."[10] Unfortunately, Carroll died before he reached the age of four.[11] His death was devastating for Mary, but she also believed that he was still with her, that he had just moved to a higher plane and was still helping her in her work as surely as her two living sons.[12]

Everis and Jay did indeed help. Mary and Anson held the enlightened view that young children should have opportunities to share in the household work so that they would respect the family as well as feel a part of it.[13] Also, as their sons grew up, Mary continued her preaching, spiritual teaching, and healing. Whenever she went out on a healing mission or to preach in another town, Anson and the boys went with her. Early on, Everis and Jay not only witnessed the healing power their mother possessed, but they were also able to see how others lived, which made them grateful for what their parents were able to provide for them.

The first trip to California

The Hayes family continued to operate their Wisconsin farm, but Anson suffered from stomach problems as well as weak lungs. Both he and Mary blamed the cold Wisconsin weather, in part, for his poor health and thought a warmer climate would be better for him. So in late 1872, they decided to spend the winter in California, visiting one of Mary's distant relatives, a Mrs. Michener. When they arrived on November 25, 1872, Mrs. Michener was living in an area called "The Haywards," now the location of Hayward, California.

Soon after their arrival, Mrs. Michener gathered her friends to hear Mary speak. As a result, the local temperance people heard of her lectures against drink and also invited her to speak. Mary, however, did not wish to be identified solely as a temperance lecturer, and she told them so. When they agreed to let her speak on her own topics, she was barraged with questions. She answered these, for the most

Mary Folsom LEFT *and Anson Hayes* RIGHT *circa 1854*

Hayes Family Collection

part, by pointing out how a lack of self-control led to all sorts of poor behavior, including drinking. Even ministers and their congregation, she asserted, were sometimes intemperate in their eating. Her lecture caused quite a stir in a trading center where the saloons were open even on Sundays.

During this visit to California, the Micheners moved to San Jose, and the Hayes family followed, renting a house on Fifth Street. There, a local spiritualist named Mr. York paid Mary a visit and asked her to lecture. As she had done in Hayward, she consented to a series of four lectures, provided she could determine the content. When she spoke, she emphasized her point of view that "noble thoughts and deeds are a source of spiritual and physical strength."[14]

While in San Jose, both Jay and Anson overindulged in the bountiful fruit of California, and both became sick with a form of typhoid. With his previous stomach problems, Anson suffered more severely. Mary attended both of them day and night, with Everis helping out as he could. By June of 1873,

Anson was well enough to return to Wisconsin, where he wanted to enroll his sons in the University of Wisconsin. He encouraged Mary to remain in California to have some time to rest. However, once her family had left, Mary headed to Santa Cruz, where she continued her lectures and healings.

A death in Wisconsin leaves Mary a widow

Back in Wisconsin, Jay and Everis worked side by side with their father in the harvest, encouraging him to avoid strenuous work. But in August, Anson had a heart attack, and Mary cancelled her engagements to return to Wisconsin as quickly as possible. She made the trip home by train, a passage that was interrupted when a band of Native Americans stopped the train. They made demands on the passengers in their native language, which none of the passengers could understand. Mary, however, noticed a woman in the group and started speaking to her in her own tongue—even though Mary, as always, had no prior knowledge of the language. As they spoke, Mary was able to determine that the group was starving, having had a bad winter and a poor spring. The passengers on the train found food in their food baskets—trains had no dining cars at that time—and fed their visitors, who then rode off.[15]

By the time Mary arrived home, Anson had sent his sons off to the university in Madison, claiming that he would be all right. In truth, his health was no better, and Mary concentrated her healing efforts on curing her husband. She manipulated his limbs to ease the swelling, but she recognized that, even though he was able to move around, his illness was fatal. Because Anson missed his sons so much, he and Mary decided to buy a house in Madison. Then his sons could live at home and be near their father while they studied. The family moved into its new house in October, just two weeks before Anson died, on October 16, 1873.

Mother and sons invest in a way of life

For the next five years, while Everis and Jay were attending school, Mary maintained a home in Madison and oversaw the farm in Waterloo.[16] The boys spent their summers on the farm, helping out as they could, but it was difficult for Mary to support two college educations at the same time. During this brief period—and only during this period—Mary did ask payment for her healings.[17] People continued to flock to the Hayes home, for Mary was now renowned as a religious person and healer. Some of them traveled long distances to be with her because she didn't want to be away from her sons. However, during the winter of 1880-81, she made an exception and ventured to Boston to continue healing work with a Mrs. Bull, whom she had begun to treat in Madison.[18] In Boston, she had the opportunity to meet the poet Henry Wadsworth Longfellow at his home.

About the same time, Mary's sons completed their studies. Everis graduated in 1879, starting a law practice in Madison. When Jay graduated the following year, he joined his brother's practice. Then, in 1882, Jay decided to take a position with Colonel John H. Knight in Bayfield, Wisconsin. Knight soon moved the practice to the frontier mining town of Ashland, Wisconsin. Without a home to go to, Jay stayed in a hotel in Ashland until Mary, concerned for her son's health and well-being, rented an apartment there to provide a more homelike atmosphere for Jay. She hired an old friend to be housekeeper for Everis, who remained in the family home in Madison.

It was in late December in 1882 when the Power told Mary that her sons should invest in land with a vast undeveloped area of iron ore. Over the years, both Mary and her sons had come to trust what the Power told Mary. When she told Jay about this latest direction, though, he wondered just how they would find the iron ore. Mary replied that a certain client of his knew the area they were to mine. Jay inquired of this client—a man named Captain N. D. Moore—who told Jay that he was, in fact, exploring for just such ore. The two struck an informal deal to allow Jay to invest in this mining exploration at the next possible opportunity.

In the meantime, the Ashland practice where Jay was working grew so large that he asked his brother to join him there. Mary purchased a house nearby for herself and her sons. And then, in 1883, they finally had their opportunity to invest with Captain Moore in what later became the Ashland mine, 40 miles east of Ashland at Ironwood, Michigan. Of course, there was the problem of where to get the money to invest. Everis and Jay solved this problem by buying a one-quarter interest in 68 acres of land for $10 per acre—or $1700 total. Using the money they had earned in their first year of practice together, Everis and Jay put their trust in Mary's spirit guide. Shortly afterward, they were able to sell the land for $5000, giving them what they needed to invest in the up-and-coming Ashland mine. Even though the mine was undeveloped when they purchased it, "the Power distinctly stated that the Ashland mine was intended for them and for their descendants, and that out of it should come all the money they would ever need."[19] For Mary's sons, the venture also marked the beginning of a lifelong practice—to own their businesses jointly.[20]

In 1884, Everis married Nettie Louisa Porter, and they went to live in the Hayes house in Ashland. The following year, Jay married Clara L. Lyon, and they, too, chose to live with Mary Hayes. Taking a bride home to live with the family was not as unusual in those days as it is today. But this choice set the trend for the future living arrangements of this family. At about the same time, as Mary herself was contemplating the family's future, she had a vision of a grove of oak trees in a fruitful valley. This vision of a beautiful, peaceful, and productive spot for her family stayed with her for many years.

The mining frontier

Explorations began at the Ashland mine in September of 1883. Meanwhile, the two brothers invested in additional mine sites in Gogebic iron range, which was to become the nation's largest iron mining area. They took an option on land near Hurley, Wisconsin, selling three-quarters of their shares to family and friends. This site became the Germania mine, which opened in 1885. They also took an option on the Caledonia mine. When the Ashland mine finally opened in 1885, Clara Hayes wrote to her parents, estimating that the mine could yield at least $500,000 worth of ore.[21]

In 1886, the entire family—Mary, her sons, and their wives—moved to a large house in Hurley, just across the border from Ironwood, Michigan. This was the heart of the iron mining frontier, with saloons that played to the men who worked in the Hayes mines. Mary naturally became concerned for the miners' welfare. She feared that they could never hope to do anything with their lives other than mining if they did not have some basic education and spiritual guidance. In January 1887, she asked her sons to gather together all the miners for a special meeting. At the meeting, she announced that she was forming a school where the miners could learn to read and write and prepare themselves for better work. She even offered free college scholarships for those who wanted them, and six men eventually went to college with her help. Of the men she and members of her family taught, many chose to stay on at the mines, taking important positions of responsibility.[22]

When the Hayes family initially moved to Hurley, they were joined by two families, the Lyons and Chynoweths, who were friends from their days in Madison, when Everis and Jay were at the university. The Lyons were now not only friends but also relatives since Jay had chosen to marry

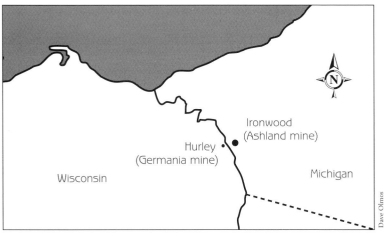

The Hayes family mines were located in the Gogebic iron range in Wisconsin and Michigan.

Clara Lyon. The Chynoweths, who built a house next to the Hayes home in Hurley, would eventually become relatives by marriage, too.

Emily and Louis Chynoweth had three children: Ellen, Louis, and Thomas. Ellen and Louis moved with the family to Hurley, but Thomas, who was considerably older than his siblings and had a successful law practice in Madison, remained behind. While working on a legal textbook, however, he found his eyesight failing. Although he had certainly heard a lot about Mary, he had never met her. His mother urged him to come to Hurley to seek Mary's healing, and he did so. That meeting was the beginning of a special bond between the two of them.

From frontier town to California oak groves

By 1887, Everis and Jay had started families of their own, and Mary decided it was time for the family to leave the boisterous mining town of Hurley in search of a more suitable, more permanent residence. The search started in Waterloo, where Mary had grown up. But the Power gave Mary no indication that this was to be the family home. Instead, the Power directed her to return to California where the family had visited for a short time the previous fall. The Power also told them to take their friends, the Chynoweths, with them.

The group toured San Diego, Los Angeles, and Santa Barbara. But nowhere did Mary find that special spot she was looking for, the place in her vision. Finally, they reached San Jose. On their last day there, just before they planned to return to Wisconsin, the Hayes brothers went out to see a property owned by John Tennant, a farmer. It was part of the old Rancho Santa Teresa land grant, six miles south of San Jose, adjacent to the Edenvale station of the Southern Pacific railroad.[23] There they saw a grove of giant oak trees, just as Mary had envisioned. They drove by carriage back into town and told her about the property. She was convinced that this, finally, was the place they were seeking.

The brothers made an offer to the Tennants, who first said that the property was not for sale and then named a price that was too high. The Tennants did, however, accept an offer of $26,000 for 210 acres across Monterey Road from the property the Hayes family really wanted. While disheartened, Mary believed that their offer would eventually be accepted, and the family set out for Wisconsin, as planned. When they arrived home, a telegram was waiting for them. It was from the Tennant family, accepting their offer of $47,500 for 239 acres, which included the Tennant family home.

Coming home to Edenvale

The next months were filled with travel between Wisconsin and California. First, Mary returned to California with Jay and Clara, as well as her sister Lucina, to take possession of the property. Then leaving Lucina behind to handle matters in California, the rest of the family returned to Wisconsin to move the family—and friends—to California. In June, the Hayes brothers sold the 210 acres they had originally purchased from John Tennant to Emily and Ellen Chynoweth for one dollar. Later, 110 acres were deeded to John Wetmore, the husband of Mary's stepdaughter, May Hayes. The remaining 100 acres were deeded to Louis Chynoweth.

By November of 1887, the entire family had returned and settled into Edenvale. Mary had been reluctant to leave Hurley because the school she had established for miners was a great success and a boon to the town. The school did remain open after she left, though. Furthermore, Mary did not entirely leave the mining community behind: shortly after the family had arrived at their new home, a group of miners and their families, fifteen in all, arrived to establish their homes at Edenvale. They simply didn't want to sever their association with Mary and her family.

By early 1888, Mary could see that the Tennant house, even with the rooms that had been added to accommodate her large family, was inadequate. So she began plans for a new house:

The Tennant house was pretty and commodious, but it did not suit Mrs. Hayes' idea of the house necessary for a large family so loving and harmonious that none of them—sons, daughters-in-law, or mother—wanted to live apart; and yet, she wished to accord to each the privileges of their own seclusion. She put herself to work mentally and physically and pretty soon contracts were out for the most elegant private estate ever erected in the Santa Clara Valley.[24]

The miners at the Germania mine near Hurley, Wisconsin, a half mile from the Ashland mine at Ironwood, Michigan

The Hayes family together at Edenvale, shortly after their arrival in 1887. FROM LEFT TO RIGHT Two unidentified women, Lucina Folsom, Mary Folsom Hayes, Everis A. Hayes holding his daughter Sibyl, Nettie Porter Hayes, Lodema Folsom Atwood, Isaac Atwood.

Hayes Family Collection

The Tennant house. It was destroyed by fire on November 14, 1938.

The family hired George W. Page as the architect. (See Chapter 2.) The house was Queen Anne in design, with more than 50 rooms. (See Chapter 3.) It was actually three residences in one—one for Mary and one for each of her two sons and their families—all connected one to another.

There was an imposing middle building for herself complete as a separate home, but, on both sides opening into the two complete houses that adjoined it, so that both of the sons and their families, while retaining the close unity essential to the happiness of all, could enjoy exclusive privileges in their own homes. There was, however, but one dining-room and kitchen. The building was superb; perfect in proportion and furnishings and of such dimensions that it required two years for its completion.[25]

At the same time the estate was being built, the Hayes family expanded their property by purchasing 158 acres of land to the west and south of the original 240 acres. For this, they paid John Higgins, the property owner, $20,000.

They also commissioned Page to design a chapel, which was constructed for $20,000 across Edenvale Avenue from the mansion in 1891. It was an elegant building:

Its audience room would seat three or four hundred people and has a fine large gallery. It is seated with proscenium chairs and in the rear of the pulpit elevation is a large bow, set with glass . . . At one side is a fine pipe organ; at the other a private entrance and passageway, which is hidden from the audience room by an intricate and costly screen of bentwood carving—a most artistic piece of work. Opening from this, and also by large sliding doors from the audience room, is the church parlor, neatly furnished and containing two grand pianos of the Steinway make. Below, the high basement is fitted up as a school room for the children or the family, and another piano for their practice is in a small room off [to the side].[26]

Marriage and death, wealth and debt

In the early years at Edenvale, it seemed that the family could do nothing but prosper, spiritually and financially. Mary found herself marrying again, this time to Thomas Chynoweth, the man whose eyesight she had healed—and whose companionship she had come to cherish. Early in 1889, Thomas Chynoweth followed his family to California, and shortly after his arrival, he asked Mary to marry him. She consented, and they were married in July of that year. She was 65, and he was 44—just 10 years older than her eldest son.

Back in Wisconsin, the mines continued to bring the family wealth. Mary and her sons returned frequently to Wisconsin and Michigan to tend to the details of operations there, including further development of the mines. Mary continued to listen for the guidance of the Power, which directed them in digging mine shafts. In 1890, when a disastrous fire started in the Germania mine, Mary directed the fire fighting efforts from California for about four months, and then finally made the long trip to Wisconsin to take a personal hand in it. Her intervention was successful, and the mine was later reopened.

In 1891, however, the family's luck began to fade. Thomas, who had always been an epileptic and of fragile health, plunged back into his law book project, believing he was healthier than he was. The effort brought on epileptic convulsions. He died on February 28, 1891, less than two years after his marriage to Mary—and months before the grand new house at Edenvale was completed.[27] Mary had little time to mourn his passing, however, because her sister-in-law, Mrs. Lyon, was desperately ill at the time and required Mary's ministrations. The following year, Everis lost his wife Nettie, who left him with three children.

Then, in April 1893, a worldwide financial panic and economic depression began. Congress had sought to lower tariffs on imported goods, including iron ore. The sharply lower labor costs in other countries would have made it impossible for Americans to sell their goods if the tariff was lowered, and the prospect stalled the sale of iron ore and generally created financial confusion. Foreign investors withdrew their capital, railroads went into bankruptcy, the stock exchange fell sharply, and unemployment climbed. For the Hayes family, the economic disruption meant that a large stockpile of ore—about 80,000 tons—went unsold. Nevertheless, they believed that the panic would end soon and continued to keep the miners working.

The Hayes chapel, designed by George Page and constructed in 1891, was located across Edenvale Avenue from the mansion. It served first as the family's private church and later as the first home of the True Life Church. It was destroyed by fire in 1903.[28]

To keep the mines operating in 1893, the stockholders borrowed money backed up by notes signed by the Hayes brothers. The family thus became liable for a debt of $650,000. For people with no experience with debt, this was quite a turn of events. In May 1893, they deeded all their property at Edenvale—except the house in which they lived—to Earl Oglebay as security against a mortgage they had secured to keep the mines running. However, in August they were forced to shut down the Germania mine. In January of the following year, they closed the Ashland mine.[29] By now, they had stockpiled 200,000 tons of iron ore. To add insult to injury, the creditors forced the Hayes brothers to resign from the boards of the two mines and took control.

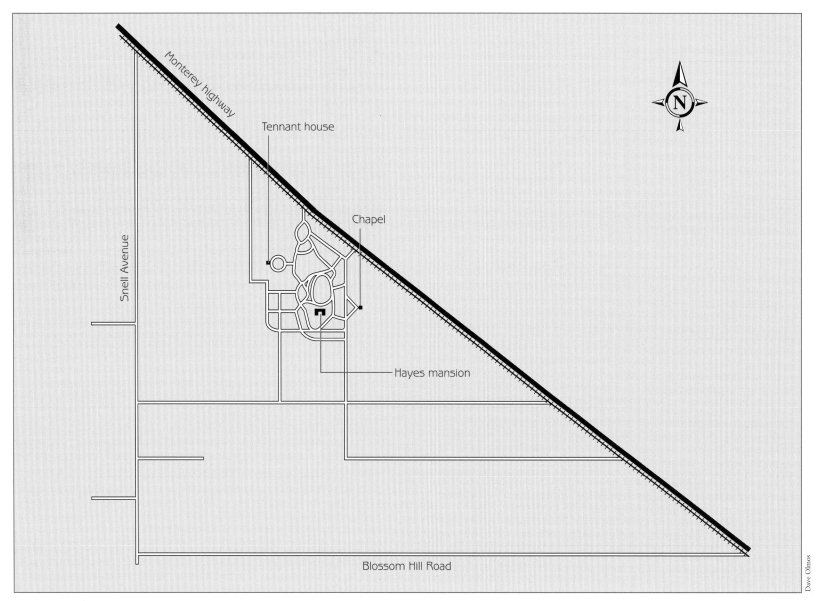

Location of the Tennant house, the new Hayes family home, and the chapel, from a U.S. Geological Survey map drawn circa 1895.

In the summer of 1894, the Hayes brothers were forced to sell the iron ore stockpile. It sold for barely enough to cover the charges of transporting it. The brothers were also forced to transfer title of the stock they owned in the mines to their creditors. By late 1895, they had mortgaged everything else they owned to pay some of their smaller creditors.

Their largest creditor was E. H. Abbot, a wealthy lawyer in Boston to whom they owed $207,000. Abbot was known as a cold-blooded businessman, but Mary directed her sons to contact him to secure a loan of $25,000 to cover some pressing debts and keep the family on its feet. Abbot advised the brothers to declare bankruptcy, which they adamantly refused to do. Finally, accepting their vows that they would keep the loan from going into the hands of their other creditors, Abbot agreed to lend them the $25,000.

Edenvale goes up in flames

From 1895 through 1897, the Hayes family kept itself together as best it could, making full use of their large farm to keep food on the table. What kept them going during those depression years was the prophecy of the Power, which assured Mary that, in the end, the family would reclaim all its property.

Finally, in 1898, the Dingley Tariff Bill passed, and business prospects brightened. By June, Mary and Jay started negotiations to regain control of the Ashland mine. They tried to secure a loan to have water pumped out of one of the mine shafts and resume mining, but this effort failed. They had to work through almost a year of negotiations before they could form a new company and regain control in June 1899.

The train station at Edenvale. FROM LEFT TO RIGHT *Unidentified man, George Hascall, Nathan Hayes, Cap Gulnac, R.F.D. carrier.*

The very next month, though, their efforts were dealt a serious blow. Their mansion at Edenvale burned to the ground. Since they had deeded their property to Earl Oglebay, they could not collect the $75,000 for which the house was insured.[30] So they moved back into the Tennant house, adding four rooms to accommodate a family of at least 15, plus several servants.[31]

Still, the Hayes family persisted. By 1900, the Germania mine was theirs once again. They regained title to the Edenvale property in 1901, paying $100,000 for it.[32] In April 1901, they sublet their mines to the Cleveland Cliffs Iron Company for an ongoing royalty fee and a large cash bonus. Once again, the family was wealthy.

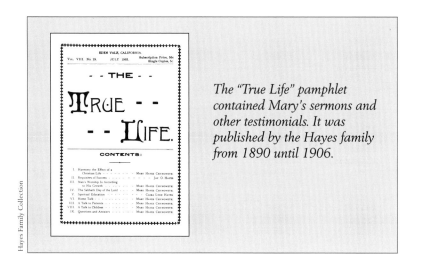

The "True Life" pamphlet contained Mary's sermons and other testimonials. It was published by the Hayes family from 1890 until 1906.

The founding of the True Life Church

During all the years when Everis and Jay were building the mining business and throughout the depression years, Mary continued to preach and heal. She did not write her sermons down beforehand. Rather, she was directed by the Power to have a stenographer present when she preached. As early as 1890, the family had begun publishing these transcriptions of her sermons in pamphlet form as "The True Life as Lived and Taught by Mary Hayes Chynoweth." The pamphlets started as a semi-monthly publication with about 200 subscribers all over the country and abroad.

Through her sermons and her writings, her fame continued to spread, and those who came to hear her urged her to form a church. Finally, on December 14, 1902, the True Life Church was formally organized in the chapel on the Hayes estate. Services continued there until May 1903, when a janitor hastily discarded a match after lighting the furnace. The church burned to the ground.[33] After that, the church was incorporated as the True Life Church of San Jose, and services were held at the Unitarian Church on St. James Square in downtown San Jose—another building designed by George Page.

In spite of the struggles through the depression years, the mines were the greatest source of the family's wealth over many years. The total ore mined from the Ashland mine alone, from 1885 until the mine closed in 1926, was seven million tons! The income from this ore—in a time when there was no income tax of any sort—allowed the family to continue to expand their mining investments as well as provide comfortably for their own needs.

Principles of the True Life Church

—From *The Spirit Dominant: A Life of Mary Hayes Chynoweth*

I. We hold that religion consists in pure and holy living and unselfish doing, and not in professions.

II. We believe in God, the Creator and Ruler of the universe, and in Him only as author of salvation for every human being, through developing Himself in each soul to the fullness of the Christ life as shown forth in the New Testament. We believe that it is the destiny of every human soul, when he so wills and labors with sufficient diligence to that end, to develop the same purity and spiritual power as Christ is represented in the Bible to have reached.

III. In order to reach that end a constant dual effort by each individual is a necessity.

First—Each must pray unto God for an increase of His life and power within him, and must desire as the chief of all valuable possessions to have incorporated in life and character all that is pure and holy in thought, word, and deed.

Second—Each must resist with all his will the promptings of his lower nature and overcome as rapidly as he can the temptations to evil.

IV. We are convinced that the Christ standard of perfection in human life is possible for each one of us and that spiritual light and wisdom come as results of growth and the overcoming of the physical elements in each nature, because of the manifestations of God's life and power which have been brought to the world through Mrs. Hayes-Chynoweth.

Among other things, she has healed the sick by laying on of hands, when no human agency could alleviate their sufferings; she has preached the gospel of God without previous study, but as the truth was given her through inspiration at the time; she reads the human heart as an open book, knows its yearnings and needs which God helps her to satisfy and supply; she has had revealed to her the whereabouts of the wealth hidden in the earth, as well as many of the mysteries of the spiritual world. God is no respecter of persons, and what He has done for Mrs. Chynoweth He will do for all of His children who work for the spiritual life with the same zeal and singleness of purpose with which she worked.

We each pledge ourselves to do all in our power to overcome the physical elements in our natures and to grow from day to day in purity and godliness; to do everything that we can to add to the interest of the meetings of this organization, and to induce as many others as possible to attend them in order that they may be benefited with ourselves.

Mary's Legacy as a Healer

Numerous recollections and accounts tell of Mary Hayes Chynoweth's skills as a healer. The people she ministered to during her lifetime count in the thousands. During the two years following her husband Thomas's death in 1891, the registry kept by the Hayes family showed that she gave over 7,000 personal treatments.*

In the late 1930s, Sibyl Hayes, Mary's granddaughter, contacted some of Mary's patients and asked for their written testimonials. The following first-person account, from Selma B. Olinder, describes the change from her initial state of disinterest in seeing Mrs. Hayes to her personal healing. It also describes how the family handled the large number of visitors Mrs. Hayes received.**

> I made the acquaintance of this remarkable woman in rather a peculiar way . . . I had not been a resident of San Jose long, perhaps a year. Next door, living as modestly as ourselves, was a Jewish family that I soon learned to regard not only with respect, but also with sincere affection. The family consisted of grandfather, daughter and her child, a girl of 10 or 11, who had some spinal affliction. This child used to go out regularly to Mrs. Hayes Chynoweth in Edenvale for treatments. At that time I had not been in good health for nearly two years because of having taken a cold, so severe that it had left me with chronic bronchitis, my right lung affected, and a badly inflamed pleura whenever I took a repeated cold which was often because of my weakened condition.

> My little friend next door became much concerned about my health, so much so that she insistently and continually begged of me to go with her to see what Mrs. Chynoweth could do for me, assuring me that it would be well enough . . . To be frank, I did not allow them to make much impression on me because of being so well entrenched in my own opinions as to my condition and what to do about it. Nevertheless the coaxing went on. I was always ready with some flimsy excuse that I considered suitable to meet wheedling, as I had come to unjustly regard it. Finally a day came when I was having an unusually serious time. I was getting desperately discouraged. As I sat for a long time in something of a deep reverie, there came to me as a voice speaking, "And a little child shall lead them." Almost as from a command, I got up immediately and went over to my little neighbor and said as I entered, "Evelyn, I've come to tell you I'm going with you out to Mrs. Chynoweth's," naming the day, whatever it would be. I need not dwell on the happy surprise of the child, but I must add, I really thought I was going to please her more than myself, for I was still the "doubting Thomas."

> We took a morning train and arrived at Edenvale early in the forenoon, not later than nine or ten o'clock. At the entrance of the home we lined up . . . as those who had appointments, and those who had not. We were given numbers accordingly. As many had arrived by horse and carriage before, I naturally found myself far down the line or list. Fortunately I had brought sandwiches, and a book to read, which with a bench in the delightful grounds of the Hayes-Chynoweth home made a perfect place in which to rest and enjoy the air and sunshine.

At exactly three I was called. For some reason or other, I did a little preening on my courage, perhaps because I had heard upon several occasions, "Mrs. Chynoweth can look right through you," so I rather favored an obtuse attitude on my part.

Upon being admitted, I chose to pause just inside the door some distance from where Mrs. Chynoweth sat, my intent gaze upon her. She suddenly looked up, regarded me rather directly for a moment, and beginning to smile said, "Why did you come?" I didn't care to tell, so I attempted some sort of evasive answer, that I realized afterward illy diverged from the point. She appeared quite amused by now, and said, "You came out of curiosity." I could neither deny or admit it for I was busy trying to "save my face." Again I parried, I thought with better success, for she said, "You are not sick," and I was, as I thought, about to take my departure, when she suddenly asked me to come nearer, around to her right side. Sensing my insincerity I am sure, she said, "Now what do you want of me?" I answered, "Anything you can tell me." Almost before I had finished my sentence she suddenly clapped her hand to her right side and exclaimed, "But you are sick, you poor thing. You need more sympathy than you ever get." For the reason, I suppose, that the ruddy complexion of my youth still lingered, I never could look very ailing.

Mrs. Chynoweth continued to skillfully trace on herself with her right hand, definitely every location where I was afflicted. One thing amazingly interesting to me was the description of a pain that I had intermittently for many years. She said, as she traced it starting over her eye, "You are better of it now, and in due time it will disappear entirely." Strange enough, when I was a child of 12 or 13 years of age, I fell one day as I was exploring a dry creek bed, and in falling struck on a rock with my forehead, the rock severely injuring me over the left eye. It left me for years with a spasmodic neuralgic pain over my left eye and down the side of my neck. All trace of it has been gone for many years, as was predicted by Mary Hayes-Chynoweth it would be.

After a most thorough and accurate diagnosis of my difficulties, she outlined for me hygenic (sic) and dietetic courses, which with some useful nature's remedies soon put me on the way to recovery. She prophesised (sic) for me a good old age if I would carry out her instructions. I did. After 45 years as principal of what [was later] known as the Selma Olinder School, I was retired last June at age 75. If the State of California hadn't gotten me, I'm sure I could have been fit for another half decade at least, even though, strange as it may seem, I was given up to die at the age of 26.

* Louisa Johnson Clay, *The Spirit Dominant: A Life of Mary Hayes Chynoweth*, p. 95.

** Letter dated January 25, 1939

Throughout her life, Mary Hayes Chynoweth was a woman of presence and power, a woman who guided others to better health and more fortuitous circumstances.

Edenvale is rebuilt, but the matriarch dies

By 1902, the Hayes family was out of debt and desperately in need of a new house. Mary turned once again to George Page. This time, she asked him to design a house of the same general plan (see Chapter 4), but of a design and material that would be as fireproof as possible.[34]

As she had in earlier times, Mary watched the building of the new house. But in late 1904, her family became increasingly alarmed that she seemed to have spells of weakness. Thinking she needed a vacation, the sons arranged a trip to Mexico City. The entire family made the trip, renting their own rail cars for sleeping and eating. For a while after their return, Mary seemed to be better, but the recovery was not permanent. She grew gradually weaker, and even a trip to the Hotel Del Monte in Monterey, made in mid-July to escape the heat of San Jose, was but a brief respite.

Mary Hayes Chynoweth died in her sleep on July 27, 1905.[35] She was 80 years old. Her last words reportedly were "I have never wronged anyone."

The Hayes brothers pursue politics and business

The Hayes family had engaged in politics from the very early years. Mary felt that religion and politics were not incompatible:

> *Politics in the Hayes family was a very live subject. "Religion and politics," Mrs. Hayes Chynoweth said many times, "Must go hand-in-hand if the community is to advance along right lights. People should not withdraw themselves into their churches and pray for strength and purity unless at the same time they exert all their influence as citizens to correct the faults in politics." She was inspired to speak frequently about political conditions, saying that the subject of spirituality embraced politics.*[36]

In a 1902 interview in the *San Francisco Examiner*, Mary is quoted as saying:

> *I advise [my sons] in politics as I advise them in all other matters. It is in politics that they need my advice most often.*[37]

In this spirit, the brothers pursued politics from an early age. From 1882 through 1883, while the family was still living in Madison, Everis served on the city council. In 1890, he was a member of the Board of Supervisors of Gogebic County, Michigan. In 1895, both brothers campaigned diligently to get McKinley elected, feeling as their mother did, that William Jennings Bryan was unfit to lead the country.

In California, the brothers first gained experience with local politics as they helped friends in a lawsuit. Corruption seemed to be everywhere, and the political bosses controlled everything, including the appointment of school teachers. Santa Clara County was long dominated by the Republican Party, which, in turn, was controlled to a great extent, by the Southern Pacific political bureau. The principal player in the political machine was John D. McKenzie, and the local political bosses operated out of the California Club, supported by the *San Jose Evening News.*[38]

Within the Republican Party, however, was a splinter group of attorneys, doctors, judges, merchants, and orchardists. In 1898, they formed the Good Government League, later renamed the Republican Good Government League. They pledged to support Republican candidates who were "pure, honest, and fearless men." Everis and Jay, both Republicans, were leaders in this league, with Jay holding the office of president until the organization dissolved in 1905. At its peak, the group had 1600 members.[39]

Understanding that the local newspapers were the mouthpieces for corrupt politicians, the Hayes brothers purchased the *San Jose Herald* in December 1900 and the *Mercury* in August 1901. They also purchased the *News* in 1942.

From the first a definite policy was pursued; everyone who so desired should have an opportunity to present his position to the public through the mouthpiece of the paper, on the condition that his cause was worthy; the publisher and editor were to decide the question or merit and importance of cause, and the honesty of the person asking the publicity. The moral tone of the paper was greatly increased, and when the Sunday editorials on spiritual subjects were made a permanent feature many people expressed their hearty commendation.[40]

Through the influence of the Hayes brothers, the league won its first major victories in the county elections of November 1898. The league did not support candidates for municipal elections until 1902, when George D. Worswick was elected mayor. He was reelected mayor in 1904. The following year, Everis himself was elected to the United

Jay O. Hayes LEFT *and Everis A. Hayes* RIGHT, *circa 1922. In younger days, the brothers were known affectionately as "Red and Black"—Jay having a red beard and Everis having a black one. Jay was 90 when he died in 1948. Everis died in 1942 at age 87.*

States Congress, where he served until 1919. During his tenure, Everis served as the ranking Republican member of the House Banking and Currency Committee and of the Immigration and Naturalization Committee. He was also active in the formation of the Federal Reserve Board. His most significant contribution to Congress was the reorganization of the rules of the House of Representatives that had originated during the long tenure of Joseph Cannon as speaker. He organized a movement against the "ironclad Cannon Rules of the House" and was chairman of the rules steering committee.

Hayes Family Collection

President Theodore Roosevelt visited San Jose on May 11, 1903.
FROM LEFT TO RIGHT *Unidentified man, Louis O'Neal, Elihu Root (United States Secretary of War), President Theodore Roosevelt, J.O. Hayes, George D. Worswick (Mayor of San Jose).*[41]

Jay was also politically active, serving on the California Republican State Central Committee from 1902 to 1935, and as a delegate-at-large to the Republican National Conventions in 1916 and 1928. He also made an unsuccessful bid for the governorship of the state of California in 1918. From 1902 to 1910 he was a member of the Executive Committee of the Republican State Central Committee. In addition, he served as a Regent for the University of California.

All this political activity was not without its problems. In 1906 and continuing into late 1907, Everis was the subject of a newspaper attack by Charles Shortridge, who published a rival newspaper, the *San Jose Times*. Among other claims, Shortridge stated that Everis was using his franking privilege

as a member of Congress to send out his own political literature and that he had deliberately burned down the 1891 mansion to collect the insurance money. Everis ignored this attack as long as he could. Finally, on October 18, 1907, he could take it no longer and brought a libel suit against Shortridge, stating the reason for his suit on the front page of the *Mercury Herald*. Over the following months, as the libel suit went to trial, the entire transcript was published in the paper. In the end, Shortridge was found guilty.[42]

In addition to their political pursuits and their publishing ventures, both brothers played significant roles in developing the fruit industry as an economic base for the Santa Clara Valley. Jay was founder (1917) and later president of the California Prune and Apricot Growers Association, now known as Sunsweet Growers, Inc.

The Hayes wives take an active role

The wives of the Hayes brothers were as active as their husbands in the community. After Nettie Porter Hayes died in 1892, Everis married Mary Louise Bassett, with whom he had three children. A gifted teacher who had taught in the public schools of Wisconsin and Colorado before her marriage, Mary had many of the same gifts and attitudes as her mother-in-law. When Everis was serving in Congress, she and the children lived with him in Washington. There, she became active in the Congressional Club, which was a women's club. She served as chairman of the entertainment committee and made particular efforts to introduce the wives of new congressmen to Washington's social scene.[43]

While Everis and Mary Hayes were in Washington, Jay's wife Clara managed the Hayes household in San Jose, and was as active in the local San Jose community as her sister-in-law was in Washington. Clara, who had earned her bachelor of science degree from the University of Wisconsin in 1876, had spent a year abroad before she married. While in Europe, she studied art and later became an accomplished landscape painter, with shows at the Stanford University Art Gallery and at San Jose Teacher's College (now San Jose State University). As a parent, she organized the Mothers' Clubs, which later became the Parent-Teacher Association of Santa Clara County. She was district president of the P.T.A. and was several times a delegate to the national convention. In addition, Clara was the representative from Santa Clara County to the Women's Board of the Panama Pacific Exposition, held in San Francisco in 1915. Over the years, she directed the Associated Charities of Santa Clara County, worked with the Traveler's Aid Society, organized the Association of Collegiate Alumni for Santa Clara County, and, in 1919, was the first woman foreman of a grand jury (for Santa Clara County, California) in the United States. She was also an active trustee in the True Life Church and wrote 25 hymns for its hymnal.[44]

LEFT *Mary Bassett Hayes, second wife of Everis A. Hayes, circa 1922. An active woman on the Washington social scene, she died in 1945.* RIGHT *Clara Lyon Hayes, wife of Jay O. Hayes, circa 1922. A mother, artist, and community supporter, she died in 1932.*[45]

New blood, new interests, new owners for Edenvale

Everis returned to San Jose from Washington in 1919, and for the next decade, the brothers co-managed their newspapers. Then, in the early 1930s, a new depression hit. This time, the family's mining interests were played out, and the brothers again had to borrow money—now against their assets in the newspaper—to keep the family enterprises going. Foreclosure on the newspaper seemed almost inevitable until 1937, when Jay's son Elystus L. Hayes became president of the newspaper company and co-publisher with Everis' son Harold C. Hayes. Times were tough, but the newspaper grew stronger as the two cousins took over the business—so much so that they were able to buy the rival *Evening News* in 1942.

Elystus L. Hayes next to a press at the San Jose News, *circa 1950. Elystus was president of the* Mercury *and the* News *from 1937 to 1952.*

The Hayes family gathers at Edenvale for the 60th wedding anniversary of Judge William P. and Adelia Lyon, parents of Clara Lyon Hayes, in 1907.[46]

However, the new Hayes generation was not able to maintain the harmony that had always characterized the early Hayes household. Friction within the family—particularly disputes about who would continue the leadership of the newspaper—eventually forced the sale of the *Mercury* and the *News*. It was purchased in 1952 by the Ridder family, who operated Northwest Publications, Inc., which later became the Knight Ridder News organization, present publishers of the *San Jose Mercury News*.

At the same time, the members of this new generation were marrying and moving away. Fewer and fewer of them lived at the Edenvale estate. Nevertheless, the family supported the house until Jay, the last of the older generation, died in 1948. Then they decided to sell. They had several proposals from interested investors, including a plan in 1953 for the county to buy the property for a retirement home. The estate was finally sold in June 1954 to three investors. But before the new owners took possession, the family gathered at their beloved mansion, one last time, to divide up the furnishings among themselves, Mary's descendants.

Thus ended seventy years of the Hayes family ownership of their beloved Edenvale estate.

Chapter 2

George Page
The Restless Architect

San Jose is a city of charming residences. Built with tasteful and modern designs, and embowered in trees and surrounded by lawns, as most of them are, they create at once a favorable impression. This is largely owing to the architects of the city, who are, for the most part, men of skill, of careful training and experience in their art. Among them is Mr. Geo. W. Page. He is devoted exclusively to his profession, allowing no extraneous matters to distract his attention. He is a member of the Masonic Order, of San Jose Lodge, No. 10, and is a popular and eminent member of society.

—H.S. Foote, *Pen Pictures from the Garden of the World, or, Santa Clara County Illustrated,* 1888.

George W. Page, 1851 to 1924, circa 1884

When Mary Hayes Chynoweth was still Mary Folsom, a young woman teaching in Wisconsin, unaware of the Power that would soon direct the rest of her life—when she was still an unmarried woman without family or visions of the mansion she would eventually erect for her family—the architect who would design that mansion was born in 1851 in Boston. His name was George W. Page, and while the details of his life would be only sparsely chronicled, his own particular vision would be preserved most elegantly in the house that Mary built.

Boston beginnings

In the 1850s, Boston was the financial and technological center of New England. It was a city steeped in its past, yet hospitable and urbane. Here, in 1851, George William Page was born to John Moses Page and his wife Diana, who were originally from Maine. John was a night watchman and would later become a Boston city policeman. George was their first son and the second of three children.[1]

No one has recorded how George spent his childhood or how he chose architecture for his vocation. But his architectural education was clearly a product of the times. In the late 1860s, most buildings were constructed by ". . . the housewright/architect [who] was, by and large, reapplying pattern book forms . . . rather than drawing upon a formal architectural education."[2] Most professional architects in the United States came from England or were Americans who had gone to England or France for formal training. Those American students who could not afford to go abroad to school followed the time-honored practice of apprenticing themselves to a master architect. The idea of an academic course of study for architects was a radical idea for the United States. Nevertheless, Boston's long heritage of engineering and architectural expertise finally spawned the nation's first school of architecture in 1867, when William R. Ware, a practicing architect, set up the School of Architecture at Massachusetts Institute of Technology. Another practicing architect, William B. Rogers, had founded M.I.T. four years earlier.[3]

Two years after the school was founded, in 1869, George Page entered the fledgling program as a special third-year student.[4] George didn't stay to finish the program, however. For unknown reasons, he left after just one year of study and sought work as a draftsman to learn the architectural trade first-hand as an apprentice.

Out in the world, George's MIT contacts served him well. From 1870 to 1875, he held positions as a draftsman at several prominent New England firms, including Bryant & Rogers and Ware & Van Brunt. He also worked at the well-known firms of Sturgis & Brigham and Hartwell & Swasey. In Boston at that time, there was no lack of work. A couple of decades earlier, a portion of the Boston Harbor known as the Back Bay area had been filled in, providing much new building space. And then in 1872, a devastating fire leveled Boston's central business district. The reconstruction kept the building trades busy, and the firms where Page worked turned out designs for churches, civic buildings, and commercial districts—as well as large homes.

A man on the move

The building industry in Boston did eventually slow, however, and George began what would be a lifetime of migration, following interesting job opportunities as they arose. His first move was to Saratoga Springs, New York, where he worked as first assistant to E. D. Harris. Harris was the architect who designed the Grand Union Hotel. Next,

George moved to Rhode Island and worked for the firm of Stone & Carpenter, which designed the Rhode Island State Prison and the Providence County courthouse.[4]

Then, in 1876, at the age of 25, George turned toward the West, making the long journey to San Francisco on the transcontinental railroad. At that time, San Francisco was the 10th largest city in the country. It was also the shipping and mercantile center for California as well as all the Pacific. Perhaps George had visited the San Francisco exposition at the 1876 Philadelphia Centennial and decided that California offered greater opportunities than Boston.

For the next two years, George continued to work as a draftsman for at least three architectural firms in San Francisco—including those of J. P. Gaynor and J. A. Reiner. He lent his hand to such distinguished projects as the new city hall and the Baldwin Hotel and Theatre.[5]

He also visited the Santa Clara Valley from time to time, and there he met the woman he would eventually marry. Her name was Mary F. Hutchinson. What could have led George to venture south to Alviso to meet her? Perhaps it was business—at that time, Alviso was an important port on the San Francisco Bay. Or perhaps the Page family knew the Hutchinson family. Both families had started out in the same county in Maine, and Robert Hutchinson (Mary's father) had run for a seat in the Maine legislature in 1843.[6] Now Robert owned several businesses in Alviso and held several political posts. Whatever the reason for George's acquaintance with the Hutchinsons, Robert was undoubtedly a source of important contacts for George in his work—as well as his personal life.

The Masonic connection

George had another source of contacts that served him well throughout his professional life—and perhaps even shaped it. This source was the Masonic order. Among architects, builders, and other professional men, the Masonic order had been an important organization from the earliest days of the new colonies in North America. A modern equivalent of the guilds formed in the Middle Ages by Masons who built the cathedrals of Europe, the Masonic order provided opportunities for businessmen to meet one another. A 20th century book on the order describes it this way:

> Although a new initiate to Freemasonry declares on his honour that he offers himself as a candidate "uninfluenced by mercenary or other unworthy motives," there can be no doubt that the majority of businessmen who become Masons do so because they believe it will assist them in business—as indeed it frequently does.[7]

No one knows when and where George joined the Masons, but it was an important connection throughout much of his life. Most major cities throughout the nation had a Masonic lodge, and as George moved from place to place, he could easily have connected with other Masons to find new business—and new business partners. He was certainly in good company. The Masons in California counted among themselves such distinguished individuals as naturalist Luther Burbank; Samuel Clemens, who wrote under the pen name of Mark Twain; Leland Stanford, who founded Stanford University; and John Augustus Sutter, of 1849 Gold Rush fame.[8]

Page designed the first Masonic Temple in Honolulu during his initial sojourn there from 1878 to 1879.

Mary Hutchinson Page, wife of George Page, circa 1884

By 1879, when George was 28, he himself must have already been a Mason of good standing. In that year, he designed his first Masonic temple in Honolulu. George, still unmarried, had journeyed there in October of the previous year, and by 1879, he was advertising himself as an architect in the local paper. The commission for the temple would not have been given to anyone but a Mason.[9]

The Masonic connection may also have been at work when, that same year, George was one of two architects invited to submit plans for a royal palace named the Iolani Palace. At that time, Hawaii was not yet a territory of the United States. It was an autonomous state, ruled by a monarch—King Kalakaua—who had become a Master Mason in November 1875.[10] George did not get the palace commission, however. He lost out to a local bricklayer-architect named Thomas Baker, a man who so bungled the job that he was eventually relieved of his post.

Coast to coast again

George did not remain long in Hawaii. By November of 1879, perhaps soured by the loss of the palace commission, he was back on board ship again, headed toward San Francisco, and then almost immediately back to his birthplace of Boston. There he went to work for an old friend, G. S. Avery, designing long blocks of residential and commercial buildings in the Back Bay.[11] He also designed the Hotel Glendon during the three years he remained in Boston. But despite the good business, George was uncomfortable in the cold Boston winters, and finally, in 1883, he returned to San Francisco—and to Mary Hutchinson.[12]

The following year, they were married and settled initially in San Francisco. George found work as a draftsman once again with architect Edward R. Swain. Then in 1886, George and his wife moved to San Jose. They were expecting their

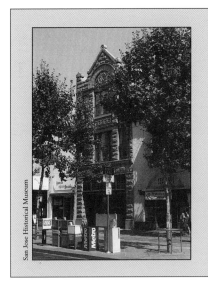

A recent photograph of the Knox-Goodrich building, 36 South First St., San Jose, the building George Page designed while he was in partnership with Edward B. Goodrich.

San Jose Historical Museum

Pen Pictures from the Garden of the World

ABOVE *Page designed this house for Los Gatos businessman John W. Lyndon in 1887. It was demolished in 1968.* BELOW *Working as an independent architect, George Page designed the Congregational Church, located at Third and San Antonio streets, in 1888.*[17]

first child, and perhaps they wanted to be closer to her family in Alviso. George set himself up as an architect once more, this time in partnership with Edward B. Goodrich, son of San Jose's pioneer architect Levi Goodrich—and a fellow mason.[13] Goodrich was the first of many partners George worked with during his lifetime.

The next years—1887 and 1888—were important for George. His daughters Gladys and Genevieve were born. He dissolved his partnership with Goodrich and didn't take on another partner until 1894.[14] Working alone, he advertised himself as "formerly in practice in an Eastern city [and] familiar with the aesthetic and economic requirements in homes for Eastern people."[15] And there occurred another event that would eventually make his reputation as an architect in San Jose: the Hayes family moved to California, settling in 1887 on their large ranch south of the city. By 1889, George was at work on plans for the first Hayes mansion. How he got the commission is unknown, but an obvious possibility comes to mind: Jay O. Hayes was also a Mason.[16]

San Jose Historical Museum

University of California, Santa Cruz

Throughout his life, Page went where the jobs were. In 1890, he designed the Sea Beach Hotel in Santa Cruz.[18]

George Page, preeminent San Jose architect

By 1891, George was setting the pace in local architecture. His work of that year was featured prominently in the *San Jose Daily Mercury* in January 1892.[19] In a special 32-page section highlighting the progress of life in Santa Clara Valley, two pages were devoted to the work of six local architects. George Page was featured on the first page, with a long biographical sketch and drawings of four buildings he had completed the previous year, including the first Hayes mansion. During 1891, George had completed nearly a quarter of a million dollars worth of buildings. These included not only the Hayes mansion but also a chapel and three other houses on the Hayes estate; a major addition to the luxurious St. James Hotel; and the First Unitarian Church on St. James Square.

The author of the *Daily Mercury* article was Francis Reid, himself an architect and subject of one of the biographical sketches. He described the local situation this way:

> *The securing of the best architectural results in our buildings will be most rapidly accomplished if the task is entrusted to local architects.*[20]

Of George Page, he wrote:

> *Mr. Page's business has steadily increased and he has attained a large measure of success, entirely by his own efforts and notwithstanding the fact of there being already in business here several architects of long residence with large circles of relatives and friends and commanding considerable influence.*[21]

Perhaps this comment is an oblique reference to George's membership in the Masons, which would have provided him with the contacts necessary to acquire his many important commissions.

The 1891 List of Credits

During 1891 George Page designed almost one-quarter of a million dollars' worth of buildings for some of the area's most influential citizens:*

Tyler Beach—St. John Street
Addition to the St. James Hotel, $60,000

G. Raggio—First Street
Brick stores and residence, $6,500

J. W. Lyndon—Los Gatos
Brick bank, stores, and offices, $16,000

Hayes-Chynoweth—Edenvale
Residence, $100,000

Hayes-Chynoweth—Edenvale
Chapel, $12,000

W. Folsom—Edenvale
House, $1,700

N. Morton—Edenvale
House, $1,200

J. Robertson—Edenvale
House, $1,500

J. Bonar—Edenvale
Residence, $1,000

Francis Smith—Bascom Road
Residence and tank house, $21,200

Francis Smith—Steven's Creek Road
Barn, $950

First Unitarian Church—Third Street
$12,000 (Still located at 160 N. Third Street)

Mr. S. M. Bruce—Stockton Avenue
Residence, $7,500

I. G. Knowles—Third Street
Residence, $6,000 (Still located at 499 N. Third Street)

T. B. Kell—San Pedro Street
Residence, $5,000 (Still located at 452 N. San Pedro St.)

O. P. Anderson—Milliken's Corners
Residence, $4,500

A. Coddington—Lewis Road
Residence, $1,500

T. S. Montgomery—First Street
Inside finishing, residence (Cost not stated)

These clients include a number of well-known and successful men of that time. John W. Lyndon was a Los Gatos businessman with property in San Jose as well as Los Gatos. Francis Smith started out as a tinsmith and wound up with a foundry in San Francisco; his San Jose home was known as Dana Farm. Thomas S. Montgomery was a businessman engaged in real estate, building, insurance, loans, and investments; the Montgomery Theatre in downtown San Jose is named after him. Lyndon and Smith were also Masons.

*San Jose Daily Mercury, January 1, 1892, p. 17.

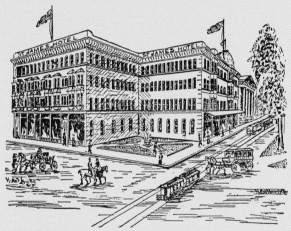

St. James Hotel,

SAN JOSE, CAL.

TYLER BEACH, Proprietor.

Elegantly Furnished with all Modern Improvements.

American Plan. Rates, $2.00 and $2.50 per day.

Rooms with Parlor and Bath extra.

SPECIAL PRICES BY THE WEEK OR MONTH.

This house now contains 225 rooms, Passenger and Freight Elevators, Electric light, Steam heat, Electric return call bell system and fire alarm.

U. S. Mail Stages leave the Hotel every morning for the great Lick Observatory. Seats reserved on receipt of letter or telegram. The table is unsurpassed. Fresh eggs, butter, milk, cream, and vegetables, are supplied fresh every morning from the proprietor's ranch.

Special attention paid to Tourists and Commercial Men.

Finest Sample Rooms in the City on Ground Floor.

This page from the 1892 San Jose city directory advertises the recently enlarged St. James Hotel. George Page designed the addition in 1891.

ABOVE One of Page's most visible and lasting accomplishments was the design of the First Unitarian Church of San Jose (1891), which still stands on St. James Square in San Jose. This photo is circa 1909.[22]

RIGHT A special section in the January 1, 1892, Mercury Herald reviewed the work of local architects and featured George Page's work prominently on the first page.

ARCHITECTURE AND THE ARCHITECTS.

WHEN WE MEAN TO BUILD,
WE FIRST SURVEY THE PLOT, THEN DRAW THE MODEL.
SHAKSPARE

LAST YEARS BUILDING RECORD

OUR ARCHITECTURE
BY FRANCIS W. REID, A.M.

Within the past few years Santa Clara county, and especially the city of San Jose, has advanced in mercantile and domestic architecture to a degree not excelled even by the extraordinary development in horticultural wealth.

The former conglomerate style of edifices due to the diversified tastes, fancies and requirements of a cosmopolitan population is being rapidly replaced by buildings characterized by stricter adherence to architectural principles.

With the increase in material wealth people have been no longer content with building mere places to live, but have erected homes. The advancement in plumbing, heating, lighting and other appliances, has enabled the house owner to incorporate many of these improvements even in homes of moderate cost, until the cottage of to-day is better equipped with sanitary and household conveniences than the mansion of ten years ago.

Esthetic and artistic ideas, sanitary precautions and domestic requirements have created a demand for the best skill in house planning and designing. Our citizens have at last realized that a home should be something more than mere rooms and walls planned and erected with reference only to utilitarian ideas. It should in its appearance and arrangement be expressive of the taste of its inmates. The exterior should be attractive and picturesque; the interior comfortable and convenient.

It is fortunate that in this county quaintness and oddity of effect is seldom desired. The extreme types of Old Colonial, Knickerbocker, Queen Anne and Eastlake have few admirers. The demand is for quieter, more refined styles. Correctness of design and suitability of exterior to natural surroundings are always admired. The blind subservience to Classical, Renaissance, Gothic, Colonial, or other modes of past civilization, will never find encouragement in our county.

Progressive ideas and the inventions of the last decade demand a better setting than is found in any architectural era of the past.

Climate also will assert its influence. Styles of dwellings that have arisen from the necessity of withstanding a temperature below zero, will always appear out of place on our streets. The manor house of England, the schloss of Germany, the chateau of Switzerland, and the colonial homes of our revolutionary fathers, are as much out of place when erected in our midst as would be the igloo of the Equimaux. Santa Clara county must select its ideas from summer regions.

Light and picturesque effects in oriel, loggia, balcony, portico, bay-window, porte cochere, turret, gable and roof line will always be desired qualities. It remains for good taste to decide the position and number of each of these, that elegance may be characterized by suitability, and the picturesque may not be marred by bizarre effects.

The greatest progress in domestic architecture is seen in our interiors. The narrow passage by courtesy called a hall, in which we only avoided the scylla of the ladder-like stairway to fall upon the charibdis of the hat-rack, has given place to the spacious reception hall, with its

elsewhere, but if its residences are unsightly, the business blocks of its city, low unornamental structures, the

region 50,000,000 feet is yearly cut. A vast amount still remains in the forest and as it is of rapid growth no famine of this valuable material is ever probable in San Jose. The kinds and grades of redwood lumber produced are legion. The wood is remarkably durable, either exposed to the weather or in contact with the earth.

Buildings erected in the early fifties are still in an excellent state of preservation, and our modern architects as a rule prefer this lumber for frame buildings and interior decoration to any of our native varieties. While the majority of the residences, both mansions and cottages, are constructed of wood, other materials are extensively employed. The business blocks are almost entirely constructed of brick and stone, excellent brick clay abounding in many localities in the immediate vicinity of the city.

For business blocks and large buildings the principal materials used are sand and brick. In fact, during the late years, all business edifices have been of this material. The stone used is generally San

Notable among the structures which have been commenced as completed during 1890, are the Jesuit College, a fine edifice of pressed brick and sandstone, on San Fernando street. A large brick addition to the St. James Hotel with large storerooms on the first floor. This fronts on St. John street. The Old Ladies' Home, a slightly frame edifice on South First street, has just been finished. Another building is being added to the Normal School for the accommodation of the Training Department, a cut and full description of which appears in this issue. The new Y. M. C. A. Building is one of the features of the city added during the past twelve months, as is also the Second Presbyterian Church, and St. Mary's Catholic Church. The former is a frame building and the latter has a foundation of San Jose sandstone, and superstructure of pressed brick. Within a few months there has been completed at the Fredericksburg Brewery a malt house, costing $300,000. The structure is of brick and stone. F. Brassy & Co. have erected extensive wine vaults on San

partial lists of the amount and character of the work done by the architects:

George William Page, Architect.

In the history of the development of all towns of note there comes a time when the village builder is replaced by the professional architect, and San Jose is no exception. It has had resident within its limits one or more representatives of that liberal profession, architecture, since the year 1849. At the present time it has, beside many carpenters and builders who can erect cheap dwellings without architects' elaborated plans, a full complement of those who practice architecture seriously, and all tastes and purses can be satisfied here.

Among others is the subject of this sketch, whose aim is to be in sympathy with the best architectural thought of the older cities in the country. Born and educated in Boston, Massachusetts, and receiving instruction in architectural history and design at the Boston Institute of Technology during 1866-1869, he served six

and the rapidly growing suburbs thereof, beside many of the business structures which went up so rapidly after the great fire in 1872.

When a dull in building operations came, he left Boston, going first to Saratoga Springs, New York State, where he was employed nearly a year as first assistant to E. D. Harris, A. T. Stewart's architect of the immense Grand Union Hotel, and other buildings there. He was employed for a time by Stone & Carpenter, architects, of Providence, Rhode Island, on the plans of the Rhode Island State Prison, and Providence County Court House, and other buildings.

In 1876 he came to California, locating in San Francisco, where he first served in the office of J. P. Gaynor. Afterwards being in the New City Hall architect's office, and the office of J. A. Remer, during the fitting up of the interior of the Baldwin Hotel and theater. At this time he paid his first visit to San Jose, met his wife (that now is) and came under the spell that usually overtakes those who

plans for King Kalakaua's palace, the plans of another architect being finally adopted. He went home to Boston in 1880, intending soon to return to the coast, but remained there three years, becoming associated in business with G. A. Avery, an old friend. Business was good, but the winters were inclement, and he could not be contented away from California, so he finally, in 1883, much against the wishes of his partner, relatives and friends, returned to this state, paying frequent visits to San Jose and vicinity, until his marriage, which took place in 1884, his bride being Miss M. F. Hutchinson. They resided in San Francisco during the year following, and then became residents of this city. He was for a year associated in business with Mr. E. B. Goodrich, son of the pioneer architect, Levi Goodrich, who retired in favor of the new firm, and soon after died during a visit to San Diego.

While associated with Mr. Goodrich, Mr. Page planned, among other buildings, the large residence of W. E. Clark, on the Alameda, being forced to work in a style foreign to all his previous or subsequent inclinations, by certain limitations, which were unsurmountable.

Mr. Page's business has steadily increased and he has attained a large measure of success, entirely by his own efforts, and notwithstanding the fact of there being already in business here several architects of long residence with large circles of relatives and friends and commanding considerable influence.

Improvements have steadily continued and increased, especially building, and numerous buildings, public and private, now exist in this city and county, besides others in Santa Cruz county and elsewhere, which have been erected from plans by and under the supervision of Mr. Page.

During the last year the fine triple country residence (illustrated elsewhere) for Mrs. Mary Hayes-Chynoweth and Messrs. E. A. and J. O. Hayes, was completed. It is in all its appointments unapproached by any other private residence in the county. It is supplied with all modern conveniences, has fifty rooms, besides halls, cellars, bath rooms, pantries, etc., is lighted throughout solely by electricity supplied by a powerful dynamo and storage batteries, is heated by hot water and is furnished throughout the greater portion with elaborate Eastern and wood finish, put together in the same manner, and finished and polished as nicely as any first-class furniture. It is also decorated with artistic frescoes, hangings and furniture, the walls in some cases covered entirely by hard wood paneling, in others by tapestries, stamped leathers and incrusta waltons.

Below are some of the buildings designed by George William Page and erected in 1891:

Tyler Beach, brick hotel, St. John street, $40,000.
G. Raggio, brick stores and residence, First street, $6000.
J. W. Lyndon, brick bank, stores and offices, Los Gatos, $16,000.
Hayes-Chynoweth, residence, Eden Vale, $100,000.
Hayes-Chynoweth, chapel, Eden Vale, $12,000.
Mr. Folcom, house, Eden Vale, $1700.
Mr. Morton, house, Eden Vale, $1900.
Mr. Robertson, house, Eden Vale, $1500.
Mr. Bonar, house, Eden Vale $1000.
Francis Smith, residence and tank house, Bascom road, $21,200.
Francis Smith, barn, Steven's Creek road, $800.
First Unitarian Church, Third street, $12,000.
Mr. S. M. Bruce, residence, Stockton avenue, $7500.
I. G. Knowles, residence, Third street, $6000.
T. S. Kell, residence, San Pedro street, $800.
O. P. Anderson, residence, Milliken's Corners $4500.
A. Coddington, residence, Lewis road, $1500.
T. S. Montgomery, inside finishing, residence, First street, cost not stated.

Theodore Lenzen.

For beautiful buildings and perfection of details, harmony throughout and superior arrangement, Theodore Lenzen has a reputation second as an architect that is equalled by few and excelled by none. Mr. Lenzen has been established in this city as professional architect since 1862, and has done much toward the improvement of the city. He was the architect of the majestic pile of building at Santa Clara College. Under his supervision was built the Auzerais House, one of the first brick structures erected in this city. He furnished the plans for the beautiful

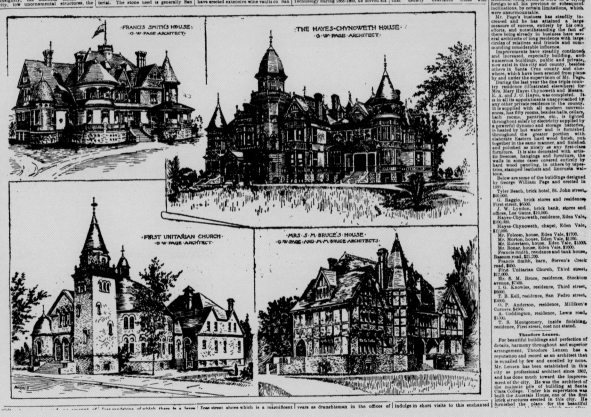

FRANCIS SMITH'S HOUSE
G. W. PAGE ARCHITECT.

THE HAYES-CHYNOWETH HOUSE
G. W. PAGE ARCHITECT.

FIRST UNITARIAN CHURCH
G. W. PAGE ARCHITECT.

MRS. S. M. BRUCE'S HOUSE
G. W. PAGE AND M. M. BRUCE ARCHITECTS.

ABOVE *The Thomas B. Kell house (1891) in San Jose is a typical Queen Anne style Victorian at the corner of San Pedro and Fox streets.* BELOW *Page's drawing of the original Hayes mansion, from the 1892* San Jose Daily Mercury *article on local architects.*

The residence for Francis Smith (1891) was located outside the city of Santa Clara, at what is now the corner of Bascom and Naglee avenues. Compare the half-round porches to those on the 1891 Hayes mansion.

New partners, a new Hayes mansion

Following this period of extraordinary productivity, George again joined in a partnership in 1894, this time with M. M. Bruce. The arrangement apparently lasted until late 1898, but no records currently exist of the buildings George designed during this time.[23] Nor is there any record of why the partners chose to go their separate ways.

George's choice was to move his family—which now included his six-year-old son Reginald, as well as his wife and two daughters—to Honolulu. For the first year of this so-journ, George was in partnership with G. A. Howard, Jr., and Robert F. Train in the firm of Howard, Train & Page. From 1900 to 1902, he was associated with Frederick W. Beardslee in the firm of Beardslee & Page, Architects and Builders.

While in Hawaii, George continued to design both homes and commercial blocks.[24] One of his drawings—a two-story business building—appeared in the local newspaper just two months before he left Hawaii to return to San Francisco. It was later constructed, as was a house for E. Faxon Bishop. Today, so little remains of Honolulu's 19th century architecture that it is almost impossible to track which old buildings did exist and where. In fact, even as early as 1910, Thrum's *Hawaiian Annual* included a special article, noting all the fine old buildings that were being torn down to feed Honolulu's appetite for expansion.[25]

The Page family returned to California in 1902, settling this time in San Francisco. While George was in Hawaii, the first Hayes mansion had burned to the ground. Perhaps Mary Hayes Chynoweth had contacted him in Honolulu to let him know that it was now time to construct her new home—for that, in fact, is what he did when he returned.

Given the size of the new mansion—64 rooms and 41,000 square feet—and considering the fact that the original required three years to design and complete, one

While in Hawaii for the second time, Page designed this house for E. Faxon Bishop. This photograph was taken in 1913. The house was demolished in 1979.

might estimate that the drawings for the new mansion took six months or more to complete. Construction probably continued over two years or more, especially to accommodate the detailed finish work inside the home. George undoubtedly would have made many trips from San Francisco to Edenvale to oversee the work.

The final project: San Jose's Masonic Temple

From 1905 until about 1915, George worked in partnership with several other local architects, including W. E. Higgins and Frank D. Wolfe (who had previously been part of the famous San Jose architectural firm of Wolfe & McKenzie). George's last major work, however, came as a direct result of his lifelong

San Jose Historical Museum

The last major work in George Page's long career was probably the Masonic Temple (1910), located on St. James Square. Today, only the facade of the Masonic Temple remains, attached to a modern building.

connection with the Masons. In 1909, he became the architect for a new Masonic temple in San Jose. Another Masonic brother, A. B. Fletcher, was the builder. The building was completed and dedicated in 1910, when George was 59.[26]

Even as he was approaching retirement age, George Page was not content to settle in one place to live out his years. He moved his residence frequently, living in several places in San Jose, Los Gatos, Mountain View, and finally in Santa Clara, near what is now Kifer Road. There he died, in 1924, his health having declined gradually over the years.

George's funeral was a testament to his lifelong membership in the Masons and his standing in Santa Clara Valley's architectural community. Among his pallbearers were Frank D. Wolfe and Charles S. McKenzie. His obituary describes him with respect and esteem:

> *Extraordinary talent, strict integrity and sterling character all contributed to the marked success of the deceased in his chosen line. He was recognized by all as a man of splendid gifts and high principles.*[27]

It is surprising how little is known today of George's life compared to those of other architects of his era, such as Theodore Lenzen. Still, the lack of fame is not necessarily a measure of his success as an architect:

> *Fame can be elusive and fleeting, of course. An architect could spend a lifetime designing many very good buildings that are functional, safe, economical and attractive, buildings that are waterproof, structurally sound, comfortable, and efficient to operate. Yet, fame may never come to such an architect, despite satisfied clients, good social connections and a remunerative practice.*[28]

Chapter 3

The First Hayes Mansion
A Queen Anne Victorian

Hayes Family Collection

The first Hayes mansion, built in 1891

The Hayes-Chynoweth residence, as it was called, was said by many competent to judge to have had no superior in the State. It was, in all its appointments unapproached by any other private residence in the county. It was supplied with all modern conveniences and had fifty rooms, besides halls, cellars, bathrooms and pantries. It was lighted throughout solely by electricity supplied by a powerful dynamo and storage batteries.

—*San Jose Daily Mercury*, July 31, 1899

When the Hayes family first arrived in San Jose in 1887, they took up residence in the existing house on the Tennant property at Edenvale. Constructed by John Tennant, it was a typical Italianate house of perhaps seven or eight rooms, built in the 1870s, and enlarged slightly when the family bought the property.[1] The house was clearly too small for three generations living under the same roof,[2] and in late 1888,[3] Mary Hayes took the first steps to rectify the situation. She called upon George Page to design a new home for the family, choosing this relative newcomer over such established San Jose architects as Theodore Lenzen and Levi Goodrich.

Design and construction of a three-family home

Neither the Hayes family nor George Page recorded any details about the design process that led to the new house. However, accounts of Mary's involvement in designing and building an earlier house in Wisconsin[4]—as well as her role in the family—suggest that it was her idea to have a triple residence.[5] The extended family was close, and they had shared the same house in Wisconsin. It probably seemed natural for them to continue this intimate lifestyle in California, while seeking some privacy for each individual family.

In addition to this special living arrangement, the Hayes family had other unusual needs that shaped the design of the house. They needed space not only for relatives to stay when they came to visit, but also for the people who came to see Mary for healing. Relatives stayed for weeks or months at a time, as travel was difficult in those days.

"Patients" also needed lodging. Instead of simply healing the people who came to her and then sending them away, Mary often took them in to teach them all the facets of spiritual and physical health. Some of these people stayed for weeks, others for months. "Auntie Wright," as she was known, was Mary's "patient" at Edenvale for more than 40 years, until her death at age 101. Those seeking help often brought friends or family members with them. Sometimes, other children were taken into the family, healed, educated, and prepared for life. With a large immediate family and with others staying for various periods of time, the Hayes household obviously had requirements beyond the norm.

So how did the planning proceed? One can only speculate. Plan books abounded in the late 1800s, and it was common at that time for a future homeowner to choose a plan from a book and have the house built without the services of an architect. Of course, for a house that would meet the needs of the Hayes family, an architect and a detailed set of custom plans were required. Nevertheless, George Page and Mary Hayes probably both consulted plan books before arriving at a final design. Perhaps the Hayes family had also seen houses that appealed to them on their trips around California and had asked George to incorporate ideas from them into their own home.

The result was a Victorian residence in Queen Anne style with approximately 22,000 square feet.[6] During the construction, Mary watched the building take shape, as she had done with the family's house in Wisconsin.[7] The design and construction took almost three years. But finally, in late 1891, Everis and his wife moved into the house, just three days before their third child was born. Then Mary and her new husband, as well as Jay and his family, moved in and occupied the third floor of their respective wings until the work on the lower floors was complete.[8]

The "footprint" of a mansion

Although the actual floor plans for the 1891 mansion are not available, it is fortunate that George Page designed both that house and the one that replaced it. On the foundation plan for the 1905 house, he marked the outline of the earlier house to show the builder where the foundation should be filled in and where it should be removed. Thus, one can clearly see the "footprint" of the 1891 house in the illustration on page 40.

The entire house rested on a foundation of stone from the nearby Goodrich Quarry. Notice in the plan that the house was shaped in a shallow U, and that the right-hand wing—which belonged to Everis Hayes and his family—was longer than the other wing. The individual family living quarters contained only sleeping and socializing areas. The kitchen and a large dining room, designed to accommodate the entire family, were in the basement.[9] Servants probably occupied the third floor.

Queen Anne style in all its glory

Virginia McAlester, in her book *A Field Guide to American Houses*, classifies houses in the Queen Anne style into four subtypes: spindlework, free classic, half-timbered, and (most common on the East coast) patterned masonry.[10] The exterior of the Hayes mansion was a glorious mixture of these types.

The front was decorated with spindled porch railings and stained glass windows in the central tower and elsewhere. Other Queen Anne elements included several styles of shingles, a variety of dormers, an array of towers (one with an unusual curved roof), half-timber detailing, and windows that

The Triple Residence Concept

What makes the original Hayes mansion, and the one that followed it, unique is the concept of a triple residence, with three separate, but related families all sharing connected living space.

Just as people do today, most young men and women at the turn of the century left home and established their own households when they married. Sometimes married children established a residence adjacent to their parents. Occasionally times they had to move in with their parents because they could not afford a home of their own. But there appear to be no other examples of a single house built as a primary residence to accommodate three separate families, all sharing part of the living space (in this case, the dining and parlor areas).

In the East, of course, wealthy families built enormous houses in the Adirondacks or at Newport, Rhode Island. But these houses were intended only for summer use. The Hayes house was designed for year-round use, and the families had no other separate residences to retreat to.

were flat, curved, square, rectangular, and oval. There were so many gables and towers that, in the view on page 37, the steep front-facing hipped roof is nearly hidden.

The ornamentation on the back side of the house, preserved in the picture of the central courtyard (page 42) was definitely more subdued than that on the front, but the typical Queen Anne elements were still there. If this house were standing today, it would be a singular and impressive example of the Queen Anne style.

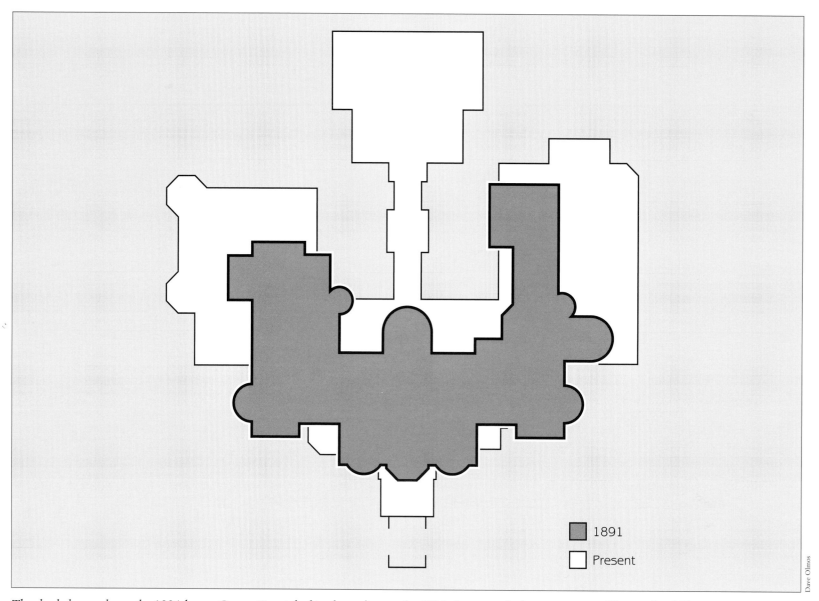

The shaded area shows the 1891 house. George Page inked in the outline on the 1905 plan to guide the contractor in filling in the old basement.

Dave Olmos

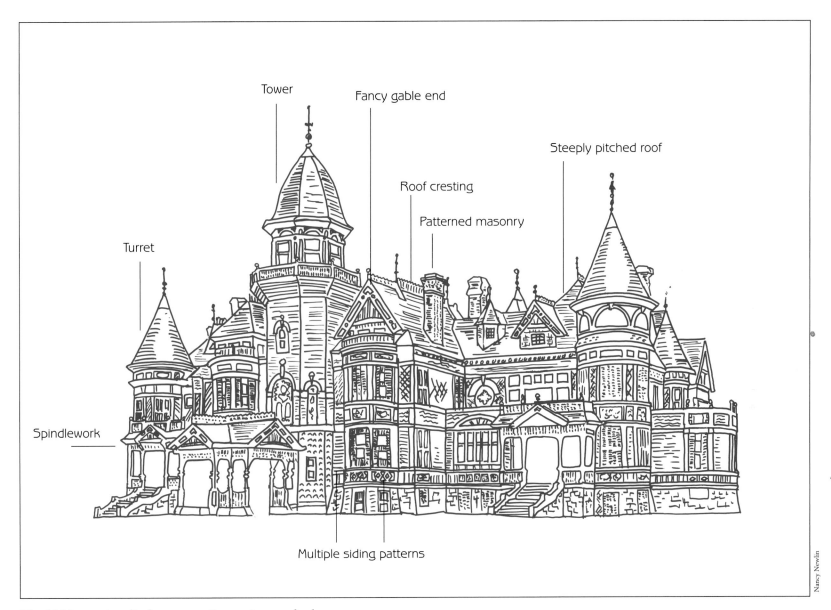

Tower

Fancy gable end

Steeply pitched roof

Roof cresting

Patterned masonry

Turret

Spindlework

Multiple siding patterns

The 1891 mansion displays many Queen Anne style elements.

Nancy Newlin

A view of the central courtyard

Modernity and elegance throughout

Consider for a minute how much this house cost to build in 1891 and how large it was. The building costs alone were $100,000. At that time, luxurious houses "in town," designed by an architect and constructed with the finest materials, might cost $8,000. Typically, such houses might have had 3,000 square feet.

Size alone did not account for the high cost to build this house, however. It was elegant throughout. The *San Jose Mercury Herald* described the interior details:

> *It was furnished throughout the greater portion with elaborate Eastern Hard Wood finish, put together in the same manner and finished and polished as nicely as any first-class furniture. Artistic frescoes decorated the walls of some apartments, while in others they were covered entirely by hard wood paneling, and in others by tapestries, stamped leathers and lincrusta walton. The furniture throughout was the most expensive to be found anywhere.[11]*

ABOVE AND RIGHT Two views of Mary Hayes' drawing room.

In spite of this elegance, photographs of the interior show restraint as well. A signature of Victorian era public rooms was a profusion of bric-a-brac of all types, from all over the world, covering every available surface. The rooms in the Hayes photographs do not have an abundance of this kind of decoration.

On the other hand, the walls, draperies, and furniture in the photographs are impressive. Wallpaper of a fine and intricate design covered each wall and was often part of the ceiling decoration as well. In some rooms, the wall covering was silk damask. The chandeliers were elegant. Sweeping

Mary's sitting room

spindled frames defined the bay windows at the ceiling and down the sides. The draperies were elegantly hung with tassels and other decoration.

The family chose typical Victorian furniture, with wood frames, damask coverings, and silk fringe. The circular settee, captured in the photograph of the Jay O. Hayes drawing room (page 44), is particularly impressive.

In Victorian era houses, the most formal and lavish area was typically the first floor, where the family entertained guests in the public rooms—parlors, dining rooms, and a drawing room, for example. Upstairs, as in the private rooms downstairs, the halls and rooms were more modestly decorated and furnished. Not so in the Hayes mansion: Mary's room was particularly elegant, but the guest bedroom certainly was not plain either.

As for utilities, the house had combination of electric and gas lights—with the electricity furnished by a dynamo and storage batteries. At that time, the electric and gas companies in San Jose and around the country were in competition to see who could capture the home lighting market. Not knowing which utility would ultimately prevail, those who could afford to installed combination fixtures. Radiators throughout the house, in addition

A guest bedroom in the Jay O. Hayes wing, with embroidered hangings just beneath the ceiling and an elegant silver bed. Notice the radiator in the corner and the velvet newspaper holder in the foreground.

The drawing room in the Jay O. Hayes wing. Notice the early painting of Mary Hayes on the stand to the left.

The sitting room in the Everis A. Hayes wing

Mary's bedroom, with a matching bed and dresser. There's ample space also for seating, and the curtained area to the left may well be a dressing room.

The kitchen, located in the basement next to the family dining room

Hayes Family Collection

to fireplaces, furnished warmth on cool winter days. Water from wells on the estate was pumped into a large tank in a tank house and fed into the house via gravity.

"Modern" amenities are also evidenced in the more mundane areas of the house, albeit on a leaner scale. The kitchen had a linoleum floor overlaid with carpet runners, a large sink with running water, and a bell system to alert the kitchen staff to attend to the family's needs.

The house burns

On July 30, 1899, at about 3:15 in the afternoon, the Hayes house caught fire. The exact origin of the fire remains unknown, but it did start somewhere on the third floor. No one was injured. Mary and her two sons were in Michigan, tending to the Ashland mine. And since it was Sunday, many of the Hayes employees were elsewhere. With much of the family and staff away, it was difficult to summon enough help to fight the fire. Those at the house attempted to get a fire engine from town, but because of the distance and the lack of fire hydrants on the estate, none was sent. By 5:30 that evening, all that remained were smoldering ashes and whatever furniture and valuables the family had managed to drag out of the house.[12]

Mary, ever philosophical about the events of her life and confident in the wisdom of her spirit guide, commented on the loss of the house in a letter dated September 2, 1899:

The house was needed for some other purpose and we needed the experience else it would not have burned. I have not felt a pang or shed a tear over the loss of the things in the house or the house itself. I have had a strong evidence that I did not worship mammon [wealth]. If it is right and best for us to have another house we may have a finer one.[13]

HAYES-CHYNOWETH MANSION TOTALLY DESTROYED BY FIRE

Flames Supposed to Have Been Started by Electric Wire Completely Consumed the Palatial Edifice.

San Jose Mercury News

A long and detailed article in the Mercury Herald *describes how the house burned. The illustration is the same one that appeared in the 1892 article on San Jose architects and George Page. (See page 33.)*

Chapter 3

Chapter 4

The Second Hayes Mansion
The Gem of Edenvale

The Hayes mansion, circa 1953

The beautiful main residence contains sixty rooms, many of which are very large, plus 12 bathrooms with many additional toilets and lavatories. The building is a unit, two wings of which were for the accommodation of the families of E. A. Hayes and J.O. Hayes, opening one into the other, connected and easily accessible. The central wing was for guests, entertaining, etc. The rear wing contains dining rooms, kitchen and rooms for employees. The front wing contains an elevator running from the basement to the third floor. The construction is very substantial. Foundations are concrete and steel. The exterior walls are brick and steel (stuccoed) and the roof is of tile.

—From a real estate brochure circa 1952

When their mansion burned in 1899, the Hayes family moved back to the original Tennant house, adding on some rooms once again to accommodate an even larger family than before. Not yet fully recovered from the financial setbacks of the '90s depression, they could not begin rebuilding their home until 1902. That—by coincidence or by design—was the year that George Page returned to San Francisco from Hawaii. It is interesting to speculate that Mary Hayes Chynoweth, now 77 years old, sent for him, asking him to design a new house for the family. After all, who would be better qualified to design the house than an architect who was already familiar with the family's needs, having designed the previous house?

The new house takes shape

One can imagine George Page, now 51, sitting down with the aging Mary and assessing the current family size, noting necessary changes to the living arrangements that were part of the 1891 house, and discussing the current styles and building methods. Again, there are no records of such discussions. But one thing is known: George had to design "a house that must not only be fireproof but [also] substantial enough to withstand an earthquake."[1] Even present-day descendents of Mary Hayes Chynoweth report that this instruction was paramount.

Judging from the size of the house—41,000 square feet—George Page must have gone to work immediately after his return from Hawaii in August to prepare plans that would allow the contract for the basement to be let in April 1903. That contract alone was for $26,000, with the foundation completed in August of that year.[2] The entire construction of the house, including the installation of all the interior woodwork, wallpaper hanging, and carpet laying, continued another two years. The family didn't move in until Thanksgiving in 1905—four months after Mary Hayes Chynoweth died.[3] The total cost was reported as $150,000.[4]

A new floor plan

As explained in Chapter 3 (page 39), the floor plan of the current house had the same general U-shape as that of the 1891 house, with a few significant differences. The front plane of the house was changed, with the two side wings moved back so that they each met the forward wing at only one point—and only on the first and second floors. Even the basements did not connect to one another. This design solved a problem in the 1891 house: there, all the residences were contiguous, allowing the fire that destroyed the house to spread rapidly.

As in the 1891 house, Mary's wing was in the center, with wings for the sons on either side—Jay's family in the east wing and Everis's family in the west wing. The rear building housed the kitchen, dining rooms, and servants' quarters. It was directly to the rear of Mary's wing and connected to it by a wide hall with a large skylight overhead. This hall was used as a conservatory.

Although floor plans for the first house do not exist (see page 40), that house reportedly had many, many rooms—50 according to one account—for its 22,000 square feet of space.[5] Such was the rule for Victorian houses. They had many small rooms with high ceilings connected by narrow hallways. The 1905 house had 64 rooms in 41,000 square feet of space, making it more open and spacious, with wide hallways and ten-foot ceilings. In addition, the house was extraordinarily light compared to most Victorian homes. Each room had many large windows. A large light well, covered by a glass skylight at the roof level and with a leaded glass light between the second and third floors,

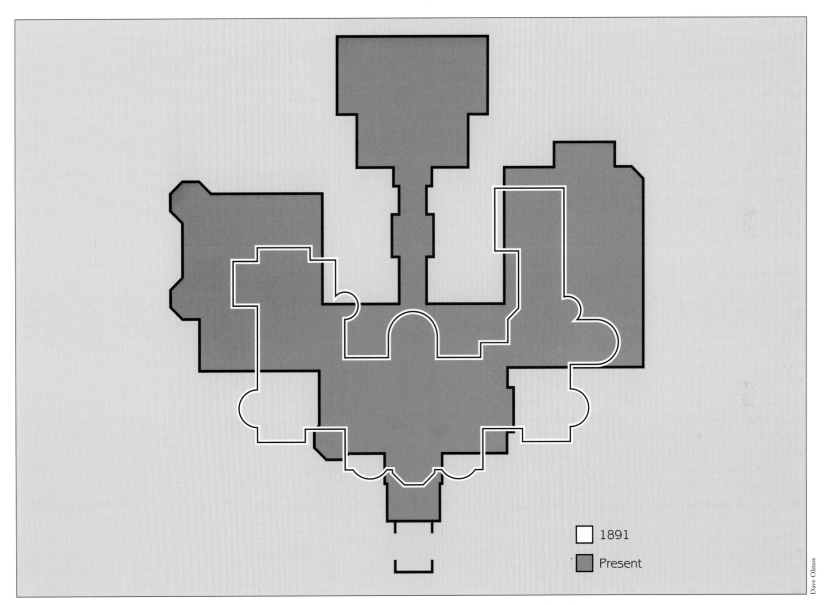

The 1905 mansion (shaded) was almost twice as large as the 1891 house (outline), but had a similar shape.

1891
Present

Dave Olmos

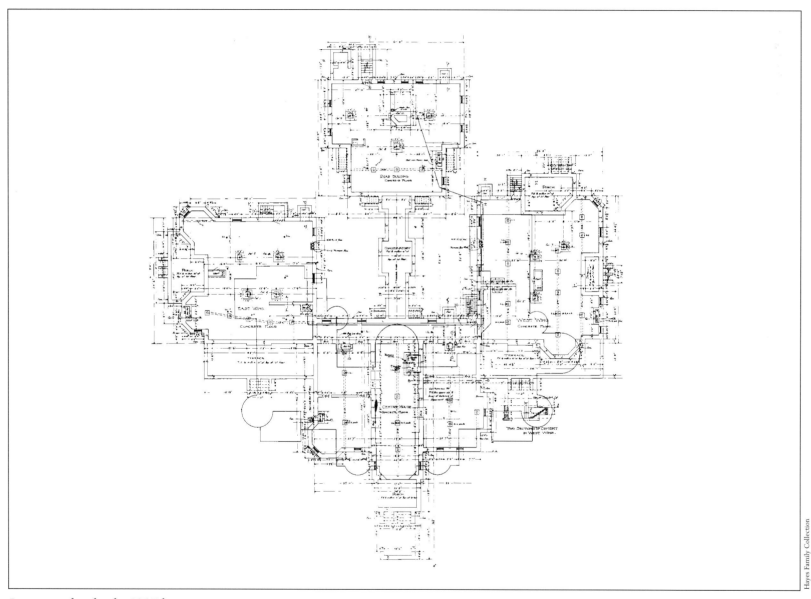

Basement plan for the 1905 house.

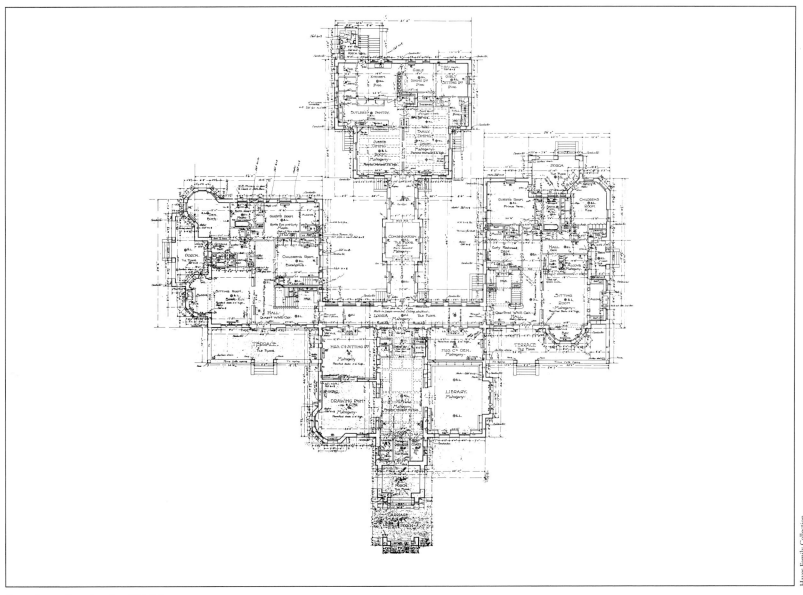

First floor plan for the 1905 house

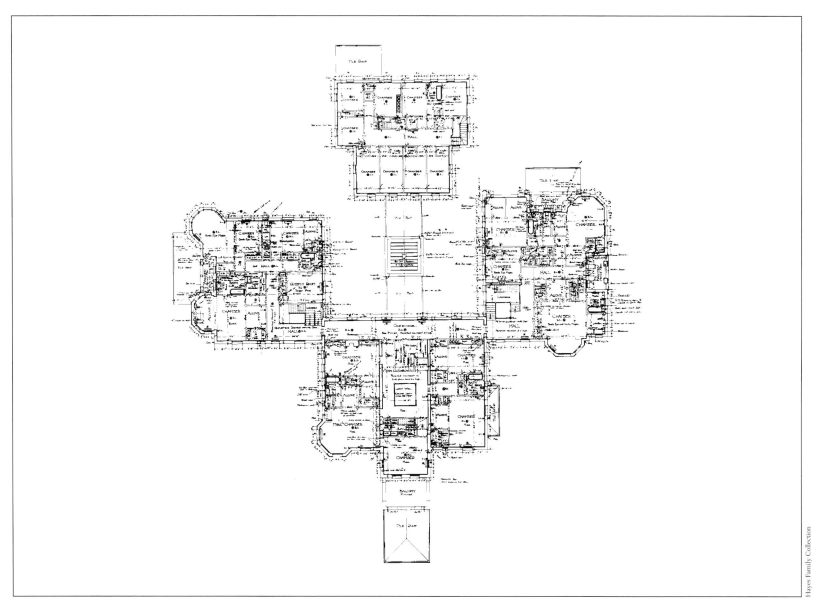

Second floor plan for the 1905 house

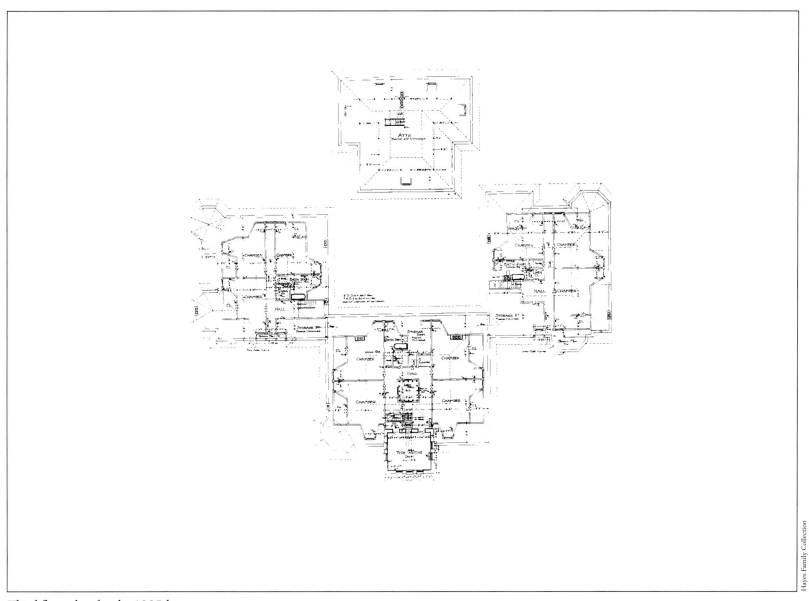

Third floor plan for the 1905 house

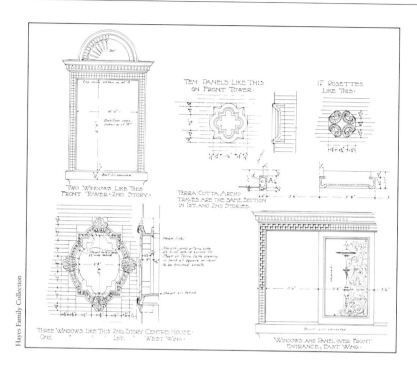

ABOVE *Part of George Page's plans for the terra cotta details*

RIGHT *Detail of terra cotta produced by Gladding McBean*

pierced all the floors of the center wing, bringing light into the main part of the house. High windows along the hallway that joined the three wings brought this light into the adjacent rooms as well. The windows and skylight in the conservatory also poured light into the house. On a sunny day, the interior glowed. This was clearly a "modern" house for 1905.

The exterior: a mix of architectural styles

The exterior design was an eclectic mix of at least three styles: Queen Anne, Mission, and Italian Revival. The Queen Anne elements included the window towers, one at the corner of the central wing and one in each family wing.[6] The stucco exterior, tall central tower, and tile roof were hallmarks of the Mission style. To further confuse any specific style identification, terra cotta produced by Gladding McBean[7] in an Italian Renaissance style was used for window and door surrounds as well as other ornamentation. The turn of the century was a time when architects experimented with many styles. It is not surprising, therefore, that Page would incorporate details of many styles in a house this large.

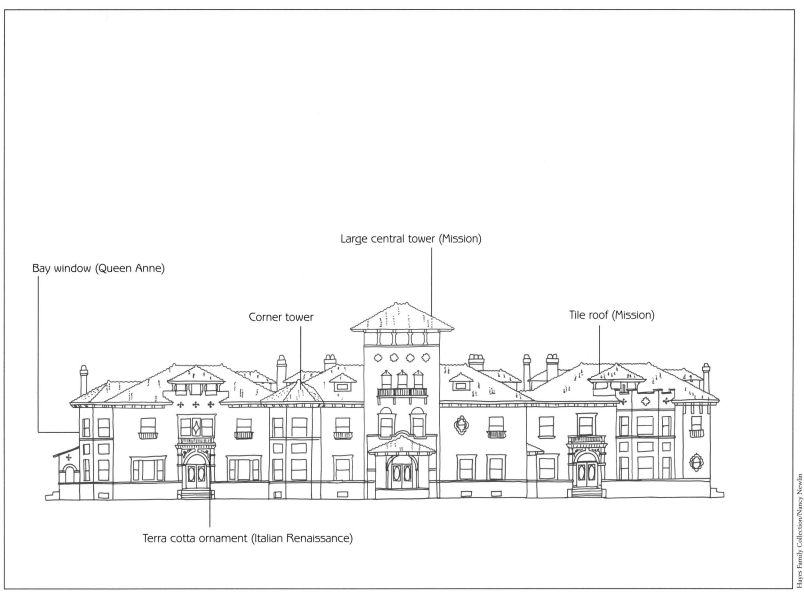

Large central tower (Mission)

Bay window (Queen Anne)

Corner tower

Tile roof (Mission)

Terra cotta ornament (Italian Renaissance)

Queen Anne, Mission, and Italian Renaissance styles are evident in the exterior of the 1905 house.

Engineering for fire prevention and control

Besides the stucco exterior and tile roof, other fire prevention and control features were built into the house. At the single point where the wings connected, each hallway could be closed with a tight-sealing copper-clad fire door. The third floor and basement in each wing did not connect with the center wing at all. The rear wing, where the kitchen was a primary source of fire, was isolated from the rest of the house by the conservatory. The major framing was done with steel columns and beams, with the exterior walls and major interior walls constructed of brick.

In the event of a fire, the family could take two measures to stop it from spreading. First, they could close the fire doors. Then, in each wing, they could use the fire hoses that were built into wall cabinets in the main hallway of the first and second floors. At one time, these hoses were connected directly to a separate water supply system because the family could not rely on fire trucks. In 1905, it was still a long drive for trucks from the San Jose fire department, and besides, there were no city fire hydrants in this area until the mid-1960s.

A day at the Hayes mansion

To get a better sense of what life was like in the Hayes mansion in its early years, you might imagine that you are a guest arriving for a visit in late 1906. You arrive at the Edenvale station by train, about a six-mile trip from San Jose. A short walk down Palm Avenue brings you to the mansion. Passing under the iron gate, you proceed to the side door of the east wing through the large screened porch to visit Jay O. Hayes, publisher of the *Mercury Herald*.

Hayes Family Collection

An early photograph of Jay O. Hayes' study in the east wing.[8]

Jay's study is around the corner. The trim in this room is maple, and you notice a double section of built-in, glass-fronted bookshelves to your left as you enter the room. The room is not entirely quiet, however. A children's playroom is down the hall, and some children are there at play. In fact, the house is bustling with activity.

The main hall in the Jay O. Hayes wing has a view of the grand staircase in this early photograph.

Sitting chairs line the loggia with its marble floor.

As you have arrived in time for dinner—which is the noon meal—you and Jay Hayes walk down the hall past the parlor and grand staircase, through the loggia paved with dark burgundy marble. You turn left and pass through the conservatory, filled with light and plants. There are actually two adjoining dining rooms, but only one is in use today as a small group assembles around one of the large round tables. Both rooms are elegantly trimmed with mahogany wainscotting and built-in cabinets. The walls are covered with tapestry panels, and the floor has a wool carpet with a blue and black geometric print.

The table is laden with bowls of food from the farm—a meat dish (with Clara Hayes grating fresh horseradish at the table), salt-rising graham bread with freshly-churned butter, potatoes, milk gravy, and chocolate or vanilla junket (pudding) for dessert. No tea or coffee is served. Conversation around the table addresses many topics, including politics—remember that Everis and his family are in Washington, D.C.

After dinner is a time for relaxation and quiet conversation, a time to settle the stomach. Passing back through the conservatory, you walk straight ahead down the main hall to the center wing, little used since Mary's death. On your right is the sitting room, and on your left, the library with case upon case of legal tomes—all protected by glass.

The front hall, with its plush carpet, heavily embossed wallpaper, and mahogany trim, is shown in this early photograph.

An early photograph of the sitting room shows how much more restrained the decoration is in this house, compared to the one built in 1891. The wall panels are covered with silk damask.

In the evening, the family assembles again for supper, a light meal compared to dinner. After supper, everyone gathers in one of the sitting rooms for an evening service. You sing a few hymns with piano accompaniment, and Jay reads a "Thought for Today" from the *Mercury Herald*. It's an excerpt from one of Mary Hayes Chynoweth's sermons and provides a harmonious way to end the day.

After the service, it's bedtime for the children. Because it's winter, fires are lit in the fireplaces, even though the house is nicely warmed by an extensive system of hot water radiators. You sit and talk with the adults in the sitting room for a while, and then find your way to the nook under the staircase, where you settle in to read a book.

Hayes Family Collection

An early photograph of the library in the center wing with glass-fronted bookcases filled with legal volumes. The white outline above is that of a white marble bust.

You are spending the night, so you retire to the guest room on the first floor. Here is a sleeping alcove with a bed, two brass wall sconces, and a curtain. The rest of the room is your sitting area. All the wood trim, including the built-in chest of drawers, is of bird's eye and curly maple—even the toilet seat in your bathroom! In the bathroom sits a large claw-foot tub, too. The walls and floor are covered in marble.

Your stay with the Hayes family ends the following morning after breakfast with a short walk back to the Edenvale station. You have conducted your business satisfactorily and enjoyed a restful and pleasant time.

Chapter 5

The Hayes Estate
An Oasis and a Working Farm

This magnificent estate, which originally comprised 600 acres, has all the beauty of an ancient and lordly English manor, and is even more extensive than many of those far-famed country seats. In its park of 40 acres one may find trees, shrubs and flowers indigenous to every clime.

—*San Jose Evening News,* July 27, 1905

The Eden Vale home was about six miles from San Jose, the nearest place from which provisions and supplies could be secured. In those pre-automobile days that was a long way to go for groceries and meat. Therefore, as far as practical, everything needed was produced on the farm.

—Clare K. Berlin, *The Hayes Family: Reminiscences of Elystus L. Hayes*

LEFT TO RIGHT *Abbie Pearson, Clara Lyon Hayes, and Ellen Chynoweth Lyon enjoy the park.*

Hayes Family Collection

When one sees the Hayes mansion in its present setting of six acres, surrounded by fences and housing, it's hard to imagine how the estate looked when the Hayes family first settled there. One sees the house, of course, and the park, which was almost as renowned as the house itself. But surrounding all that were hundreds of acres of orchards and fields: a large working farm.

A formal park in the midst of a farm

One of the first things the Hayes family did when they settled on the Edenvale estate was to set aside 40 acres for a formal park, just north of the mansion. From the front of the house, the family could step out onto a broad sweep of lawn with a view into the trees and the park beyond. As Mary's grandchildren grew, the front lawn became a perfect place to have a baseball or football game on a Sunday afternoon after dinner.

The family hired Rudolph Ulrich, designer of the gardens at the Hotel Del Monte in Monterey, to design the park. The result was a rolling area with a stream and several "gardens within a garden." Blooming plants—violets, geraniums, and Scotch heather—covered large areas. Scattered throughout the park were ponderosa pine, pepper, Italian cypress, and black locust. Palm, cedar, and eucalyptus trees lined paths that were wide enough to drive a wagon or automobile on. In fact, what is now Edenvale Avenue was once called Palm Avenue for the palms that were planted on either side. The street was renamed after the palm trees died from lack of regular watering.

The park became widely known for its beauty. Although not a public park in the present sense of the word, the gate was always left open so that people could visit. Mary's patients could also wander around in this restful setting as they awaited their turn to see her. In nice weather, groups

Hayes Family Collection

LEFT TO RIGHT Jay O. Hayes, Lena Lindeman, Abbie Pearson, *Mildred Hayes, Clara Lyon Hayes, an unidentified woman, Ellen Chynoweth Lyon, and William P. Lyon, Jr., relax on the lawn in front of the house with a view of the park beyond.*

would gather here for picnics, and the Hayes family, too, enjoyed picnics in their park.

A description of the gardens at the Hotel Del Monte gives some idea of the kind of garden Ulrich designed for the Hayes family:

The same magnificence characteristic of the hotel is repeated in the grounds, which comprise one hundred and forty acres, laid out in lawns, flower gardens, parks and groves . . . The natural trees, principally pines, and the beautiful California live-oak, have been left as nearly in a state of nature as possible, and where art has been applied to them it has been

Mildred Hayes LEFT *and Abbie Pearson, Mary Hayes Chynoweth's last secretary* RIGHT, *on Palm Avenue*

ABOVE AND BELOW *Two views of the park at Edenvale*[2]

> *done so skillfully and adroitly that the result is an innocent fraud perpetuated upon the beholder who believes he sees only nature. The landscape gardening is a marvel of beauty.*[1]

The area around the house was beautifully planted as well:

> *An evergreen bower, inclosing [sic] flower beds in many designs, occupies a portion of the space between the residence site and the road front.*[3]

Later, other special gardens were added to the grounds, including a walled-in rock garden just to the southeast of the Jay O. Hayes wing.

Hayes Family Collection

A large gathering, probably of the Hayes family, in the park for a picnic. Notice that fruit crates are used for seating.

How the Estate Was Acquired

1887	(April) Hayes family purchases 210 acres from John Tennant, north of Monterey Road.
1887	(May) Hayes family purchases an additional 239 acres from John Tennant, south of Monterey Road and including the Tennant family home.
1887	(June) Hayes family "sells" the original 210-acre purchase to Emily and Ellen Chynoweth for $1.
1888	Hayes family purchases 158 acres from John Higgins.
pre-1903	Hayes family purchases 310 acres from John Stock.

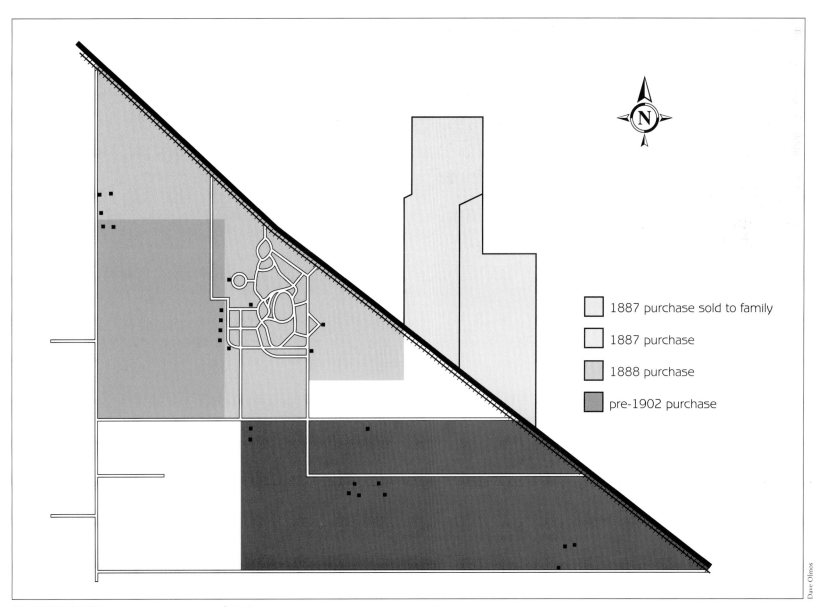

By 1903, the Hayes estate encompassed 646 acres.

1887 purchase sold to family

1887 purchase

1888 purchase

pre-1902 purchase

The carriage barn, built in 1887, had stalls for the horses, carriage storage, and sleeping rooms for the stable hands.

The architecture of a farm

While the Hayes mansion was the "gem" of Edenvale, the working farm required many other structures, some of which predated even the original 1891 home. For example, in 1887, the Hayes family built the first of many buildings on the property, a stylish new carriage and horse barn for $10,000. It had "every appointment for the housing and comfort of fine driving horses"[4] as well as five sleeping rooms for the

In the lath house, young plants could make the transition from the greenhouse to the grounds.

stable hands. It was probably the most impressive structure of its type in the area and certainly a rival for Leland Stanford's famous stable on the Stanford University campus. In later years, when automobiles took over for carriages, the building served as a garage until a separate one was built.

A large work barn had stalls for horses and mules and served as a storage place for the farm equipment. Cows were milked there, and hay was stored in the loft. A separate granary stored farm produce such as wheat and dried fruit.

Planting on the grounds went on almost without interruption, so two glassed-in greenhouses were built with an adjoining lath house. Here plants could be started and gradually moved outdoors.

In several poultry houses on the farm, hens, geese, and turkeys were raised. Other fowl—such as peacocks, pheasants, and guinea hens—were allowed to range through the barnyard.

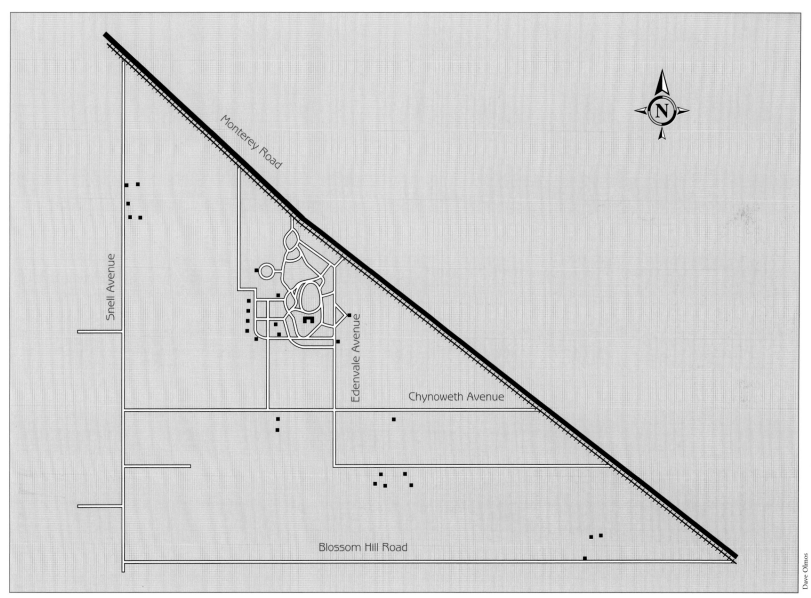

By 1895, at least 28 structures stood on the Hayes estate.

The Edenvale orchard in bloom

Animals and growing plants need water, and to supply this water, the family built a water tower and tank house. In the early years, a windmill pumped the water from wells to be stored in large water tanks in the tall tank house. Later, gasoline-driven pumps replaced the windmill.

All of these buildings supported a large farming operation. Much of the land was covered by orchards, pastures, and pens for the livestock, as well as fields for growing hay, oats, barley, wheat, and alfalfa. Of the vast acreage, 180 acres were planted as orchards. Prunes and apricots were raised commercially, with 140 acres of prunes planted in 1889.[5]

During harvest, the prunes were allowed to ripen and fall to the ground where they were gathered up, taken to a shed, and dipped in preserving solution. They were then laid on trays in the sun to dry. Finally, the dried prunes were put in sacks and taken to the packing house.

Apricots were picked ripe, taken to a cutting shed to be cut and pitted, then set out on trays to be placed in a shed and exposed to sulphur fumes. Afterward, they were set out to dry. While most of the apricots were dried, some were canned on a large stove in the basement of the rear wing for the family's own use.

To support the dried fruit operation, the family built a packing house near the Edenvale train station. Other local farmers brought their dried fruit there to be repacked in containers for shipment to the East. This operation became the basis for the family's interest in the Santa Clara Valley dried fruit industry and was a steady source of additional income. Jay, himself, was instrumental in forming the cooperative that later became Sunsweet Growers, Inc.

In addition to the dried fruits and grains, a wide variety of other food crops were also grown. Among the fruit crops were peaches, pears, cherries, apples, figs, dates, oranges, lemons, and grapefruit, as well as a wide variety of berries: strawberries, blackberries, gooseberries, and loganberries, to name a few. Almond, English walnut, black walnut, pecan, and chestnut trees were planted. Vegetable crops included peas, corn, beets, lima beans, carrots, cauliflower, eggplant, potatoes, garlic, artichokes, lettuce, squash, and horseradish.

All the family's food needs—from meat to fruit to vegetable—were supplied by these farming operations. And through the years, Mary's own grandchildren worked alongside the other farm workers, taking on such tasks as harvesting the hay and cutting dried fruit.

Everything from bunk house to schoolhouse

A variety of other buildings were also needed to support the farm and the Hayes household. For example, a boarding house and bunk house were home to the large crew of men needed to tend to the orchards, fields, gardens, and park and to care for the animals. The boarding house provided a kitchen and eating area for these men, who were well fed in accordance with Mary's dietary prescriptions.

Another building was the woodshed. Every winter, one or more trees would fall or have to be removed. The trees were sawed into manageable lengths and taken to the woodshed where the large pieces were sawed into shorter lengths and split by hand. Everis spent many hours chopping wood for exercise, and most of the Mary's grandchildren took a turn as well. After all, there were 11 fireplaces in the house to keep supplied with wood!

In 1891, the same year that the first Hayes mansion was constructed, George Page designed four other houses to be built on the property. These each cost between $1,000 and $1,700 to construct.[6] One was home to William Folsom, Mary's brother. The others were built for James Robertson, the farm manager, and for Nels Morton and James Bonar, the orchardists.

The estate even had its own schoolhouse. In the beginning, the basement of the chapel was used as a schoolhouse for the Hayes grandchildren and other children of estate workers. After the chapel burned in 1903, a schoolhouse was constructed near the old Tennant house, to be used while the present house was under construction. Eventually, however, most of the Hayes grandchildren took the train into San Jose to go to Washburn School, a private school located on San Pedro street about three blocks from the train station.

The 12-car garage was constructed of stones from the foundation of the burned-out chapel.

Finally, there was the garage. In 1906, the Hayes family purchased its first car, a Columbia Locomobile. Eventually, Jay's daughter Lyetta purchased a Pierce Arrow. This car called for a garage, and one was built of stones from the foundation of the chapel that had burned. Located about one-quarter mile west of the house, it was topped with red tiles and could house 12 cars.

Over the years, as the estate passed from owner to owner, and as large portions of the property were sold for development, the farm buildings were destroyed. (See Chapter 6 for details.) Today, all that remains of the glorious Edenvale estate is the mansion and the weed-filled Edenvale Garden Park, former site of the Hayes family's magnificent park.

Chapter 6

The Gem is Polished

The Hayes Renaissance Conference Center

The Hayes Renaissance Conference Center

It is understood that to "restore" the residence to its original opulence in every sense is not realistic for economic reasons. It is more important and prudent to rehabilitate the building for a new use that will maintain its former dignity while supporting its continued use and preservation.

—Hayes Mansion, San Jose, California,
   published by the City of San Jose, circa 1991

After the Hayes family sold their estate in 1954, the property passed from hand to hand for nearly thirty years, with each new owner unable to find the perfect use for it, many unappreciative of its inherent value. Several investors tried several schemes—from low-income housing to condominiums to an alcohol rehabilitation center to a restaurant and hotel. One owner even hoped to convert the mansion to a funeral home and the grounds to a cemetery. In the end, it took a neighborhood preservation group, some good friends on San Jose's City Council, and a development team with the right experience and vision to polish an old gem like the Hayes mansion and turn it into the Hayes Renaissance Conference Center.

The mansion languishes, the neighbors rally

As a succession of investors struggled, without success, to profit from the Hayes estate, the land and house both suffered. In 1959, a grass fire on the property destroyed two abandoned barns and a concrete block building and damaged the interiors of four other buildings. That same year, 40 acres of the estate was sold for development as Frontier Village, an amusement park for children that operated until 1980. In 1973, firefighters responded to a fire on the second floor by breaking a hole in the roof and destroying the leaded glass skylight between the second and third floors. Rainwater began leaking in, damaging the interior further.

As the mansion languished, its neighbors looked on with dismay. Scheme after scheme for the mansion fizzled, and residents became alarmed that the mansion, in an ever worsening state of disrepair, would soon reach a point where it would have to be torn down. Led by Lilyann Brannon, they decided to intercede: they formed the Save the Hayes Mansion Committee.

The Hayes mansion in 1989. For three decades, the mansion suffered neglect and even vandalism.

Their first effort was to secure legal protection for the mansion. They accomplished this goal in 1975 when the City of San Jose, which had annexed the Edenvale property in 1963, got the mansion listed in the National Register of Historic Places. Their efforts also caught the attention and enthusiasm of Judy Stabile, who was then an aide to San Jose City Council member Jerry Estruth, in whose district the mansion was located. In 1979, when the City Council voted to allow a developer to build condominiums on the Frontier Village property, Jerry was the dissenting vote. The condominium project failed, but that same year, Bren Corporation began building houses on 43 acres on the south side of the estate.

The threat of this kind of development propelled the neighbors to form the Eden Vale Historic District Committee the following year. The committee petitioned to form an historical district to offer further protection to the mansion. The effort failed, but it generated enough interest to have the mansion and 6.2 acres designated a San Jose City Landmark.

A fire in the upper hall of the front wing in the late 1970s resulted in severe damage to the area, including the loss of the leaded glass skylight and water damage from holes chopped in the roof to quench the fire.

The city takes the torch

Then in 1983, the Redevelopment Agency of the City of San Jose[1] purchased the mansion for $1.5 million, with the intention of turning it into condominiums. The neighbors were appalled. So were Judy and Jerry. When Jerry decided not to run for the City Council the next year, he encouraged Judy to run in his place. She was elected and immediately went to work to try to prevent the conversion of the mansion into condominiums. Her first step was to invite Mayor Tom McEnery, a longtime friend of historic preservation, to tour the mansion—and to propose that the city purchase the property. In 1985, the city did just that. Later, it also bought the Frontier Village site for a city park.

By 1988, Judy was busy persuading the Santa Clara Valley chapter of the American Institute of Architects to organize a design assistance team that could develop guidelines to assist the city in evaluating proposed development plans. The team met for a year, joined by community representatives, members of the Hayes family, local development companies and technical consultants as well as the staff of various departments in the City of San Jose—and, of course, by Judy and her staff. This study pointed toward two possible scenarios: a culinary/cultural complex and a conference center. The study was submitted to the City Council in 1990. A request for proposals—known in development circles as an "RFP"—went out in June 1991.

Judy and other San Jose city officials sat back now and waited for developers to respond. Fortunately, they didn't have long to wait. Jeff Davenport, of the Renaissance Conference Company in Santa Clara, was alerted to the project by his real estate manager and finance director, Grant Sedgewick, who had received a copy of the RFP. Jeff met with Judy at the mansion and immediately saw the potential.

Davenport's plan

With his background in helping create the Chaminade Conference Center in Santa Cruz—plus three years of successful and growing business with the Renaissance Meeting Center at TECHMART in Santa Clara—Jeff recognized the business opportunity at the Hayes estate:

> After Judy and I got out of our cars, I just stood and looked at the mansion, and there was silence for what seemed to be five minutes. Finally, she said, "Well, what do you think?" I said, "I know exactly what we need to do with this house." She asked, "Well, what is it?" I said, "We're going to turn it into a conference center."[2]

Jeff saw that the secluded setting would enhance the draw for the conference center business and that, when completed, it would also be a unique location for weddings and special events. With state-of-the-art audio-visual equipment installed, the mansion would be a money-maker for the Renaissance Conference Company as well as an asset to the city. He also saw the down side: he would be taking on a large and difficult project, dealing with a house suffering from years of neglect and water damage and with neighbors who weren't necessarily in agreement about a new use. Nonetheless, he began work immediately.

First, Jeff contacted Bill Ryan of Barry Swenson Builder, a local builder/developer. Ryan had been responsible for developing the detailed cost estimates in the RFP, and now he joined Davenport in the development proposal. The Renaissance Conference Company was selected as the developer, as well as the lessee and operator of the conference center. The proposal included excavation of the courtyard area between the two wings to add an underground meeting room. Another larger meeting room was to be constructed underground, east of the kitchen wing, with a plaza above it. The kitchen wing would be expanded to the south. Over the conservatory, a large, glass-enclosed atrium would provide a dining area. The plan called for business meetings during the week and special events in the evenings and on weekends. In addition, a bar and restaurant would be available to the public.

The team's first hurdle was to convince the City of San Jose that it was a viable development team. Jeff Davenport and the Renaissance Conference Company brought a growing conference center business and a skilled and experienced management team. Barry Swenson Builder brought a long history of large and successful historic restoration and renovation projects in San Jose—including the De Anza

Hotel—and a long-standing involvement in the project. Both parties were also local, making it easier for city officials to evaluate them and the conference center business in general. As officials grew more comfortable with the long-term prospects for the project, the team grew more confident that the finished project would indeed net the return necessary to make it successful.

Barry Swenson Builder and the Renaissance Conference Company thus were chosen as the project team in late 1991, with Barry Swenson Builder also selected as the contractor.

Making the dream come alive

After weeks of discussion, during which Jeff and Deputy City Manager Dan McFadden came to agree on the deal, financing the project became the biggest hurdle. The first tack was to sell limited partnerships (investment shares) in the project, with the incentive of the 25 percent tax credit for historic rehabilitation. After a short while, however, it became clear that this process would take a long time to net enough money for the project. In addition, the cost of borrowing such a large sum would be high.

Dan realized that, with a solid and capable development team in place, it was crucial to find funding for the project so that it could move forward quickly and not lose momentum due to funding problems. In addition, Judy, who had championed the Hayes mansion for more than 10 years, was leaving office in January 1992, and her special project would likely falter without her influence on the city council. Dan decided that, to get the project going, a special deal was needed: the city would have to provide 90 percent of the funding, and the private development team would then provide 10 percent.

A Short History of the Conference Center Industry

The history of conference centers as free-standing locations where people can hold meetings away from their usual place of business begins in 1950. In that year, Columbia University renovated a house on the Harriman estates north of New York City into the Arden House. This was also the first use of an historical structure for a conference center. In this case, however, the university had exclusive use of the property.

The first conference center developed by a private business was the Tarrytown House in Tarrytown, New York. Previously the Mary Duke Biddle and King estates, this facility opened in 1964 and was an instant success. It was followed in 1968 by the Harrison House of Glen Cove, New York, and the Harrison House of Lake Bluff, Illinois, both developed by Harrison, a conference center development and management company.

The purpose of a dedicated conference center is to provide a facility exclusively for meetings, in a setting away from the business site. Further, it should provide an optimum physical environment, including state-of-the-art audio-visual equipment, lighting and environmental controls, and food service.

A local example of a conference center created from an historic building is the Chaminade Conference Center in Santa Cruz, developed on the site of a boy's high school built by the Marianist order in 1930. The Hayes Renaissance Conference Center is only the second conference center in the State of California incorporating an historic building.

Benefits to the City of San Jose

The unique public/private agreement to fund the Hayes Renaissance Conference Center provided some key benefits for the city:

- An aging but historic building got a new lease on life.
- The city retained ownership, while the Hayes Renaissance Limited Partnership assumed responsibility for the debt service, maintenance, repair, and all operating costs.
- The building could function as a focus for the area, greatly improving the neighborhood and giving the community a place to hold special events.
- The development would complement plans for a proposed Edenvale industrial park.
- A portion of the profits from the conference center was earmarked to renovate Edenvale Park, former site of the Hayes family's renowned garden park, which had been failing since Frontier Village vacated the site.
- A portion of the profits was set aside for long-term building maintenance.
- The public would have access to the restaurant facilities and historical photograph galleries in the main hallways, as well as guided tours on Sundays.
- The city and community would have free access to meeting room space for a specified number of days per year.

When the final construction costs of $12 million were determined, Mayor Susan Hammer and the San Jose City Council unanimously approved a bond sale for the city portion of the development costs. The Renaissance Conference Company, along with the Green Valley Corporation and Gradeway Corporation, formed the Hayes Renaissance Limited Partnership for the private portion. A deal was born!

As the financing was coming together, the project architect, Dennis Meidinger, A.I.A., was hard at work developing the final plans. Dennis had worked with Jeff Davenport on the development of the Renaissance Meeting Center at TECHMART. His challenge in this project was to make the new use fit into the old space. A baseline requirement was to retain the main corridor system, the dining rooms, the staircases in each wing, and the rooms on the first floor of the front wing. Other rooms could then be combined by eliminating walls to form rooms in a variety of sizes appropriate for the conference center's business needs.

Meanwhile, other members of the development team were working through the various city approval processes. Jeff initially estimated that the project would take two to five years to get off the ground, considering all the city requirements that needed to be met, including rezoning. However, as the project reached the point where other city departments would be involved, it was able to take advantage of a streamlined development process the city had just put in place in their recent bid to attract the San Francisco Giants to build a stadium in the area. The stadium project failed to come together, but the team concept was already in place in the city. Dan reactivated the team for the Hayes mansion project, saving countless hours over the long run. Thus, the key city departments—the City Attorney, Public Works, and Planning—and the development team could all clearly see and discuss what had to be done to keep the project moving toward a final development proposal and contract. With this team approach, the approval process required only three months—probably about one-third the time one would expect for a project of this size and impact.

A small glitch along the way

A key component of the financing package was the 25 percent rehabilitation tax credit for the private investors. To secure this tax credit, the project had to meet the Secretary of the Interior's guidelines for rehabilitation because the building was listed on the National Register of Historic Places. These guidelines delineate such requirements as compatible use, preservation of the distinguishing character of the building, and the percentage of the walls that can be removed. Four governmental entities had to approve the plans: the city planning department and other city offices; the city Historic Landmarks Commission; the California State Historic Preservation Office (SHPO); and the National Park Service (as the arm of the U.S. Department of the Interior) to ensure that the building remained on the National Register of Historic Places and thus qualified for the investment tax credits.

As he developed the design, Dennis carefully tracked the crucial variables using his computer-aided design (CAD) system. The plans easily won the local approvals, and the developers met with SHPO to confirm that their plans would meet the historic preservation standards. SHPO's role was to okay the plans to justify the tax credits and the project for the Park Service review. All seemed well with the project as it was reviewed by a contract architect hired by SHPO—until the final plans were submitted. After a long delay without a final clearance, the chief architect at SHPO gave an emphatic thumbs down to the atrium design, citing its incompatibility with the original building and multiple points of contact with the historic structure. Judy was furious, the development team was enraged and dismayed, and the project came to a sudden halt.

It didn't die, however. Judy stepped in to assist the development team in getting more specifics from SHPO about alternatives that might be more acceptable. Then Dennis went back to his plans with the new directive to remove the atrium and to design instead an addition that would contain the large meeting room, kitchen, and dining room. With the CAD technology, he was able to redraw the plans within a few weeks—compared to the three months of work it would have taken to redraw them by hand. Then the plans went back through all the approval processes.

In the end, the alternative design worked out well in the financial plan. While the project incurred extra costs for the redesign, the new structure was far easier and less costly to build than the underground structure originally planned. The new plan also eliminated some of the uncertainties surrounding the technologically unique atrium structure.

Dennis Meidinger, A.I.A.:
George Page's Work in Retrospect

Dennis Meidinger, A.I.A., was the architect of the renovation that converted the Hayes mansion into the Hayes Renaissance Conference Center. In the course of his work on the project, he had an opportunity to see the original mansion torn down to its core structure. Commenting about his predecessor's work, he said:[3]

> I think Page did a good job making the building earthquake-resistant. Because it's an unreinforced masonry building, I thought a steel superstructure would be required to hold up the building when I first saw it. However, the shear values (horizontal strength) of the bond between the brick and mortar in the brick walls was good enough that, in combination with California's historic building code guidelines, we could count the wall strength as part of our structural analysis. Therefore, no steel superstructure was required, which significantly reduced the complexity and cost of the construction. The quality of the construction overall made the renovation far less costly.

> One thing I find particularly fascinating is the heavy-duty, commercial-grade items that Page specified: one-quarter inch glass in the windows, chains instead of ropes in the window pulleys, and metal instead of wood lath for the plaster. At the time the mansion was constructed, average residences were not built this way. I've only seen these details in commercial buildings of the era. I theorize that Page applied his experience designing commercial structures to the Hayes mansion.

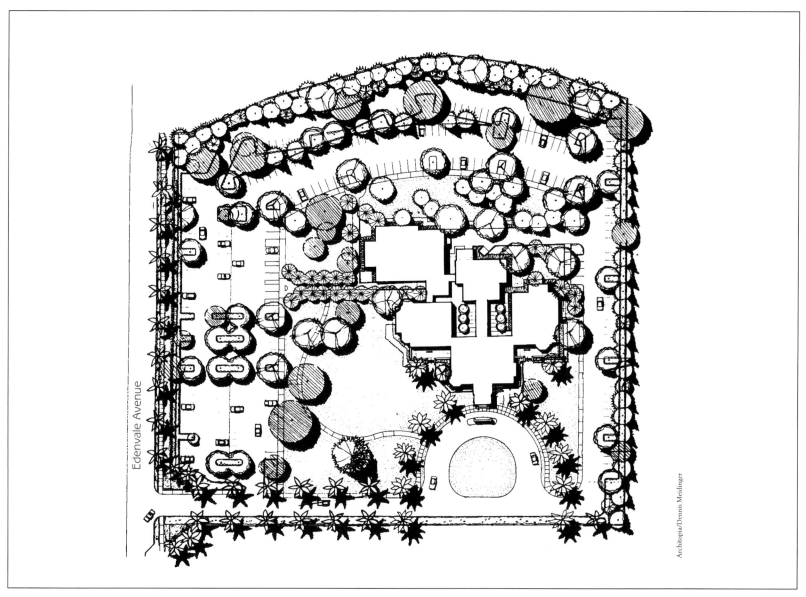

Edenvale Avenue

Architopia/Dennis Meidinger

Site plan for the Hayes Renaissance Conference Center

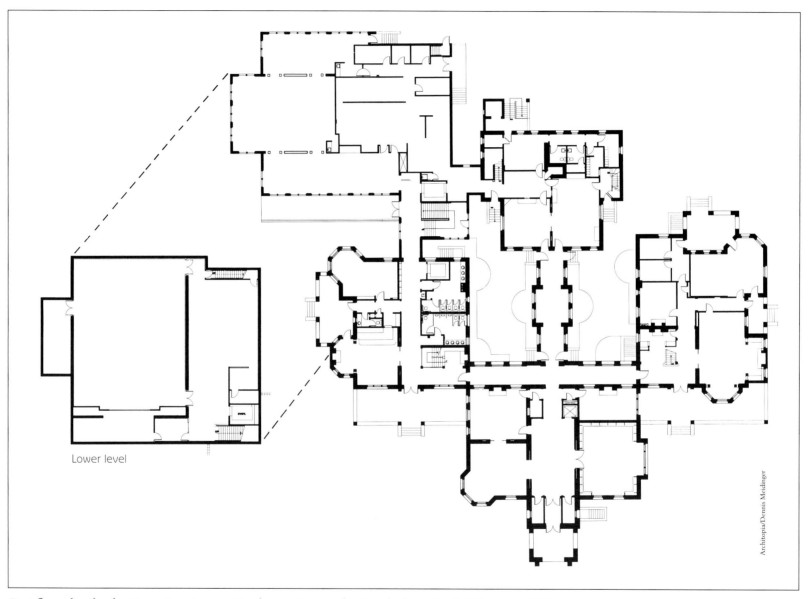

First floor plan for the Hayes Renaissance Conference Center, showing the lower level of the new addition

Lower level

Architopia/Dennis Meidinger

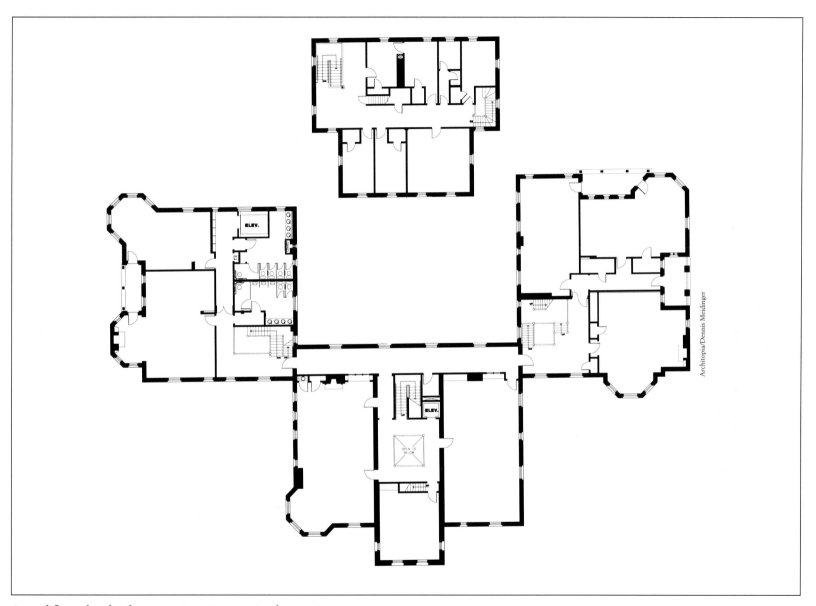

Second floor plan for the Hayes Renaissance Conference Center

Judy Stabile: Matron Saint of the Hayes Mansion

Jeff Davenport fondly refers to former San Jose City Council member Judy Stabile as "the matron saint of the Hayes mansion." Stabile first saw the mansion in 1973 and drove by it nearly every day for the following 20 years. For her, the building had an air of mystery around it. Its size was imposing, and its location so far from the city center and surrounded (eventually) by housing was an anomaly. When she first became interested in the mansion, Judy had a full-time job and volunteered time to the League of Women Voters. There she met Judi Henderson, and the two of them eventually became docents at the San Jose Historical Museum, realizing that they shared a keen interest in local history.

Judy's personal involvement with the mansion began in 1980 when caretaker Velma Lisher, in conjunction with a neighborhood group led by Lilyann Brannon, offered tours of the mansion to drum up interest in preserving the structure. "When I saw the sign out front offering tours one day as I was driving by, I screeched to a halt and drove up," she recalls. "As soon as I went inside, I was impressed by the size and complexity of the building as well as by its elegant and beautiful woodwork. I was 'hooked.' After the tour, I left with a petition to pass around to my neighbors."[4] The petition drive, while successful in gathering the required number of signatures, did not result in the formation of an historical district.

That same year, Jerry Estruth became the council member for District 2, then located in the vicinity of the San Jose airport. When the city was redistricted shortly thereafter, District 2 became the Edenvale area. Unfamiliar with the area, Jerry hired Judy as his analyst to assist him in understanding the needs of his new district. Under her influence, he developed an interest in the Hayes mansion, as well, and began to seek ways for the city to purchase and preserve it.

In 1981, Judy joined her old friend Judi Henderson on the Historic Landmarks Commission, serving until 1984. This experience gave both women a more in-depth look at historical structures throughout the city and led them to form a partnership to work on saving the Hayes mansion.

Meanwhile, in 1983, Jerry Estruth decided not to run for reelection to the city council and persuaded Judy to run. She came to office in January 1984, bringing in Judi Henderson as one of her aides. At that time, the Redevelopment Agency was just presenting its plan for converting the mansion to low-cost housing. Judy persuaded Mayor Tom McEnery to put off the hearing until she could look more closely at the project. Her involvement at this crucial point in the mansion's history eventually led to the abandonment of the housing project, the city's purchase of the mansion, an AIA Task Force, and, finally, to the Hayes Renaissance Conference Center project.

The east stairway was protected by carpet and plywood during the demolition.

ABOVE *Doors and trim are stacked in a room ready for reinstallation.*
BELOW *Plaster and walls are removed.*

Preparing for reconstruction

The construction project began in June 1993 with a demolition phase, which started in the basements, proceeding to the east wing and then counter-clockwise through the building to the west wing. Simultaneously, demolition got underway in the south wing. Prior to the demolition, key woodwork features that were not going to be altered in the renovation were protected by layers of padding.

The demolition process consisted of removing all light and bathroom fixtures, built-in cabinets, marble panels in the bathrooms, doors and door trim, selected walls, the ceilings, the elevator, and all the wiring and plumbing. All doors, door frames, wood trim, and light fixtures that were removed were identified and cataloged, so they could later be matched to their original location. Then walls were removed to create larger rooms, or plaster was taken down

Floor joists were bolted to the brick walls.

so the walls could be reworked. All the ceilings were re-moved and lowered 12 inches to allow for the installation of electrical wiring, plumbing, and ventilation.

During this demolition phase, the contractors discovered some "secrets" of the building. For example, all the wood trim was not one type of solid wood. Instead, it was constructed of layers of wood. The door frames have an inner core of redwood and an outer sheathing of one-quarter inch of some exotic wood, such as curly maple. The doors, door frames, and cabinets may have been built elsewhere, shipped to the Edenvale site, and then assembled.

On the exterior, outside stairways that had been installed to meet code when the property was a drug and alcohol rehabilitation center were torn down, and some trees were removed from the grounds. The old swimming pool was dug out and the space filled in. Two holding tanks for rainwater runoff were also dug up, removed, and the spaces filled.

Reconstruction

Reconstruction proceeded on several fronts at once. On the inside, the basements were upgraded for seismic safety. Seismic reinforcement was a major project in the building. All the brick walls had to be tied into the floor joists, to prevent lateral or horizontal movement. Holes were drilled through the joists and into the brick walls. Large bolts were then glued in with epoxy cement, and the washer and nut secured the joist to the wall.

Then work followed the same pattern around the building as the demolition had. New walls were constructed, and plumbing and electrical wiring was installed. Next, sheet rock was installed for new ceilings and walls, a preformed cove was installed between the wall and ceiling, and the ceiling and walls were plastered.

At the same time, crews were busy on the exterior reconstruction as well. Their tasks included reconstruction of the soffits, roof repairs, construction and installation of soffit vents, and an exterior primer. Large cracks had to be injected with epoxy. Then a primer and final coat of paint were applied.

Once reconstruction was complete, the door frames and doors were reinstalled, baseboard trim was recut and rein-stalled, and trim that had been protected during the construction was revealed. Where enough old trim was not available, new trim was cut to match and installed. Wall coverings were installed, lights were rehung, the carpet was laid and new draperies went up.

On the grounds, more crews removed old driveways and paved new ones, as well as walks and parking lots. They brought in trees and constructed new "sound walls" to reduce noise in the surrounding residential neighborhood.

ABOVE New gypsum board and preformed cornices were installed in a ceiling. *BELOW* A construction worker repairs the soffits.

Owls Call the Mansion "Home"

During reconstruction of the exterior, some soffit panels were removed for replacement and repair. As a construction worker on a cherry picker was reinstalling a panel at the front of the building, a barn owl flew out from under the eave, right past him. Looking into the vacated space with a mirror and light, the worker discovered a nest with three eggs and two hatchlings. The contractor's on-site crew called Joan Priest, director of the wildlife division for the Humane Society of Santa Clara Valley. She came out with a special box, went up on the cherry-picker, removed the nest, and took the birds back to the Humane Society. The area was left open for several days so that the female would realize that the nest was gone and vacate the area.

The three eggs eventually hatched and the five baby birds were raised at the Humane Society with an adult owl that had a broken wing. Bob Schlick, of Barry Swenson Builder, the contractor's on-site supervisor, became interested in the baby birds and called Joan for owl house plans. He constructed the nesting boxes according to her instructions and installed them in trees in Edenvale Garden Park. When the babies were old enough to be relocated, they and the adult bird moved into to the bird houses in the park. Construction workers on the site reported that they frequently saw the birds in the area.

ABOVE A workman installs marble that was removed from the old bathrooms and recut for the fireplace hearth. BELOW Old baseboard is recut and installed.

Reusing Old Mansion Components

When the Hayes mansion was renovated, many components that were removed before the construction began were re-used. Doors, door frames, wainscotting, and baseboards were returned to the site and reinstalled. Lighting fixtures were polished and rewired. Missing pieces were recast. Door knobs, hinges, and escutcheons (the plates on the door underneath the door handle) were polished and renovated or cast anew. Large panels of blue-veined marble removed from the bathrooms were polished and recut to be used around the fireplaces and for bathroom sinktops.

The final efforts

As work concluded on the exterior of the east and south wings, construction began on the new wing, a 15,000-square-foot addition incorporating a large meeting space, kitchen, and dining room. This wing was connected to the south and east wings by a walkway, fulfilling the historic preservation requirement that new construction contact the old building in only two places. With the construction complete and the furniture in place, the gem of Edenvale was ready to take on a new life.

Today, rooms that were once home to a large and close-knit family are now the site of corporate meetings. With the addition of a large meeting room and full kitchen, the estate has become an inviting venue for weddings and large dinner meetings. Even these changes, though, are much in the generous spirit of Mary Hayes Chynoweth. Through the house she envisioned, she continues to offer a peaceful and elegant setting for the entire community to work and celebrate the events of their lives.

ABOVE *The upper hall of the front wing, once charred by fire (see page 75), is now refurbished and has a new stairwell to the third floor.* BELOW *One of the light fixtures that was polished, rewired, and reinstalled.*

ABOVE *The east stairwell, with new carpet and its wood refinished, is ready for someone to sit by the fireplace and read.*

Nancy Newlin

A Chronology of Decline and Preservation

1953   Santa Clara County supervisors investigate the possibility of turning the mansion into a county hospital for chronically ill patients.

1954   The mansion and its remaining 131 acres are purchased by four separate investors for $250,000. The investors are Benjamin Smith of Los Altos; Day & Young, a Santa Clara fruit processor; Joseph Kiser Corporation of San Jose; and Jack DeBell of Gilroy, a subdivision developer. DeBell plans to develop the 40-acre park area into a housing subdivision with houses priced in the range of $25,000 to $50,000. The firm of Day & Young purchase 40 acres for strawberries and row crops. Benjamin Smith retains title to the mansion and 10 acres around it. Kiser Corporation plans to raise strawberries on its 41 acres.

1955   DeBell sells the 40-acre park to someone who intends to use it as a 2,500 plot cemetery. The plans never become a reality.

1956   Dr. Stanley Lourdeaux, a Los Altos physician, buys the mansion in foreclosure for $20,000. He proposes converting the mansion into bachelor apartments for students taking courses at the newly constructed IBM plant nearby.

1959   The 40-acre park is purchased by Frontier Village, Inc., for use as an amusement park.

1959   Dr. Lourdeaux sells the mansion to Reverend Virgil Swope and his wife for $150,000. They intend to construct a swimming pool, convert the basement into a recreation area with bowling lanes, and turn the rest of the house into a swanky hotel and restaurant—a project they estimate will cost $100,000.

1959   A grass fire destroys two barns and the interiors of four other buildings.

1960   Swope constructs a swimming pool east of the house.

1961   Frontier Village opens.

1963   The property is annexed by the City of San Jose.

1964   The real estate agent who is trying to sell the property for Dr. Lordeaux proposes that the county purchase it for a vocational school. The proposal never becomes a project.

1971   The San Jose Rescue Mission buys the mansion and uses it for an alcoholism rehabilitation center. To comply with the City of San Jose building code, they construct four outside stairways from the second floor.

1973   A fire breaks out on the second floor near the elevator in the center wing. The fire department breaks a hole in the tile roof, destroying the skylight between the second and third floors. As a result, the roof leaks for many years, further damaging the interior.

1975   The mansion is listed in the National Register of Historic Places.

1977   A fire damages a fireplace in the suite built for Mary Hayes Chynoweth.

1979   Bren Corporation purchases 43 acres on the south side of the mansion and begins building homes.

1979   Velma Lisher, who was a caretaker resident of the mansion for Dr. Lourdeaux and who did much over the years to prevent further deterioration of the property through her personal efforts, prepares an Historic Preservation Grant-in-Aid proposal. Her plan is to acquire the mansion and rehabilitate it as housing for senior citizens and the handicapped.

1979   The San Jose City Council, with member Jerry Estruth dissenting, decides to allow a developer to build condominiums on the Frontier Village property as long as the mansion is rehabilitated and preserved as an historical resource.

by 1980   A drive-in theatre opens to the west of the mansion.

1980   Frontier Village closes.

1980   Neighbors form the Eden Vale Historic District Committee. Their mission is to persuade the city to form an historical district to offer further protection for the mansion. This action fails.

1980   The mansion is proposed as the home for the California Country & Western Hall of Fame.

1981   Judy Stabile is chosen to serve on the San Jose Historic Landmarks Commission.

1981   The City of San Jose Historic Landmarks Commission has the mansion declared a city landmark.

1983   The Redevelopment Agency of the City of San Jose purchases the mansion for $1.5 million. The purchase money comes from a fund for low- and moderate-income housing, with plans to build 88 units on the property. The neighbors object strenuously, even though Stabile points out that this development grant is the only city money available to save the building from potential demolition, despite its historic status.

1984   Vandals break into the mansion and damage some cabinets and windows.

1984   Jerry Estruth decides not to run for city council again and encourages his aide, Judy Stabile, to run.

1985   Stabile asks for and receives permission to postpone the hearing for approval of the Redevelopment Agency's plans to turn the mansion into condominiums until she can look for other alternatives. Mayor Tom McEnery agrees to the delay.

1985   The City of San Jose purchases the mansion for $2.5 million and immediately proceeds to seek developers who are interested in developing the mansion for an alternate use.

1986   A federal tax reform bill threatens to wipe out the historic preservation tax incentives, a key ingredient in interesting a developer in the property. Finally, word comes that the mansion is one of 15 historic properties around the country that is exempt from the tax bill changes.

1987   Several development proposals are submitted and rejected for financing problems and the lack of public access.

1987   The City of San Jose purchases the old Frontier Village park property for $4.5 million to make it a park and enhance the possibilities for development of the mansion.

1987   The city's Department of Recreation, Parks, and Community Services is designated as the mansion's caretaker, and increased security is provided with additional fencing and on-site caretakers.

1988   Council member Stabile persuades the Santa Clara Valley chapter of the American Institute of Architects to organize a design assistance team to do what the city cannot afford to do—develop guidelines to assist the city in evaluating proposed development plans. Two final documents are produced: a booklet that describes two alternate scenarios and a technical appendix that details the studies of the mechanical, traffic, and other improvements required.

1990   The AIA study is submitted to the City Council and immediately approved.

1991   In June, the City Department of Economic Development issues a Request for Proposals (RFP) and advertises it nationwide. Council member Stabile and her staff conduct several tours for potential developers.

1991   In September, Barry Swenson, Builder and the Renaissance Conference Company submit a joint development proposal to turn the mansion into a premier meeting center and restaurant in two phases. The first phase calls for the renovation and reworking of the interior into conference rooms with the addition of a 2,800 square foot meeting room. The second phase calls for the construction of 75 guest rooms.

1991   In October, the City of San Jose enters into exclusive negotiations with the joint developers.

1992   In August, developers submit the first round of plans for neighborhood review.

1993   In June, construction begins on the Hayes Renaissance Conference Center, with financing from both the City of San Jose and the Hayes Renaissance Limited Partnership.

1994   In June, construction is complete and the Hayes mansion reopens as the Hayes Renaissance Conference Center.

Notes

Chapter 1: Mary Hayes Chynoweth

1 Louisa Johnson Clay, *The Spirit Dominant: A Life of Mary Hayes Chynoweth*. San Jose: Mercury Herald Company, n.d., p. 17.

2 Clay, p. 112.

3 Clay, p. 13.

4 Clay, p. 22.

5 *New York: A Guide to the Empire State*. New York: Oxford, 1940, p. 18.

6 Clara Lyon Hayes, *Mary Hayes Chynoweth: A Spiritual Life*. Unpublished manuscript, 1964, p. 3. Clara was Jay Orley Hayes's wife.

7 Clay, p. 25–26.

8 Clay, p. 31.

9 There are numerous accounts of Mary's healings in the book by Louisa Johnson Clay as well as in the book by Clara Lyon Hayes. See other notes in this chapter for the complete references.

10 Clay, p. 38.

11 No official death record for Charles Carroll Hayes is recorded in the State of Wisconsin, so the cause of death remains unknown.

12 Clay, p. 38.

13 Clare Berlin, *The Hayes Family: Reminiscences of Elystus L. Hayes*. Unpublished manuscript, 1971, p. 41.

14 Clay, p. 43.

15 Berlin, p. 63.

16 Berlin, p. 67.

17 Clay, p. 43.

18 It is interesting to speculate whether Mary might have met architect George Page during this visit, thus paving the way for their future association. In 1879, Page had returned to San Francisco from a rather disappointing sojourn in Honolulu. He went directly back to Boston in 1880 and was there until 1883.

19 Clay, p. 64.

20 Berlin, p. 30.

21 Berlin, p. 95.

22 Clay, p. 78.

23 Over the years, a story has been popularized that Mary Hayes chose the name Edenvale for her home. While the name certainly fits what the Hayes family made of their estate, Mary did not choose it. When John Tennant owned the property his location was identified as "at Edenvale," to signify that he lived close to the Edenvale train station. Over the years, the estate has been referred to as Edenvale. There is no information available that specifically states who named the Southern Pacific stations.

24 Clay, p. 84.

25 Clay, p. 84.

26 *San Jose Daily Mercury*, July 27, 1905, p. 5.

27 The only mention of Thomas Chynoweth's death in the local papers is a small death notice on March 2, 1891. It states that the visiting would be at the Edenvale house. There was no larger obituary statement and no mention of Chynoweth's connection with the Hayes family.

28 This photograph was taken by Edwin A. Leach, a Los Gatos, California, photographer. Because the shrubbery around the chapel is so modest in size compared to other photographs of the building, the author suspects that this is an early photograph. Leach was first listed in the city directory in 1894.

29 Clay, p. 100–101.

30 Just who owned the Edenvale property and received the insurance money when the house burned was later the subject of a 1907 libel suit that Everis brought against local newspaperman Charles Shortridge. See note 41.

31 *San Jose Mercury*, November 15, 1938, p. 1.

32 Clay, p. 108.

33 A one-third replica of the chapel, built of stone taken from the chapel foundation, is located in the Rancho Santa Teresa Mobile Estates on the site where the original chapel was situated. It was completed in 1969 and is open to the public.

34 See Chapter 5 for details on this house, which is still standing.

35 The official cause of death was asthma complicated by old age. Mary Hayes Chynoweth was buried in Oak Hill Cemetery (San Jose).

36 Hayes, p. 178.

37 *San Francisco Examiner*, December 19, 1902, page 7.

38 David W. Eakins, editor, *Businessmen and Municipal Reform: A Study of Ideals and Practice in San Jose and Santa Cruz, 1896–1916*. San Jose: Sourisseau Academy for State and Local History, San Jose State University Original Research in Santa Clara County History, Student Publication No. 1, 1976, p. 4–5.

39 Hayes, p. 178.

40 Hayes, p. 180. The newspapers became a vehicle to spread Mary's religious philosophy. Each Sunday sermon was published the following Monday, and excerpts appeared as a daily "Thought for Today" for about 35 years. In addition, Sibyl Hayes, Everis' eldest child, taped her grandmother's sermons for broadcast on first one and later three California radio stations from 1954 to 1968. After Sibyl's death, Mary's great-granddaughter, Clare Berlin, continued airing the tapes until 1980.

41 A popular local story is that presidents McKinley, Theodore Roosevelt, and Hoover visited Edenvale. McKinley visited San Jose in 1901 and Roosevelt in 1903, but newspaper accounts of the visits do not include any mention of a visit to Edenvale. Hoover may well have visited before he was president, because he lived for a while at Stanford University.

42 *San Jose Daily Mercury*: October 18, 1907, p.1; October 29, 1907, p. 1; October 30, 1907, p. 1; November 5, 1907, p. 1; April 5, 1908, p. 1; and April 8, 1908, p. 1.

43 Eugene T. Sawyer, *History of Santa Clara County California*. Los Angeles: Historic Record Company, 1922, p. 530.

44 Sawyer, p. 905.

45 These photographs are unnumbered plates from Sawyer.

46 Back row, left to right: Sibyl Hayes, Francis P. Latimer, Elmira Skitt, Janice Phelps Latimer, Eunice Noble, Julia Phelps, Susie Wegg Smith, unidentified man, Clara Lyon Hayes, Mildred Hayes, William P. Lyon, Jr., Ellen Chynoweth Lyon, Frances Phelps, Prof. Charles King, Will Moore, Molly Moore, unidentified woman. Middle row, seated, left to right: Sarah Andrews, Catherine Northrup, Miriam Hayes, William P. Lyon, Adelia Lyon, Verosha Wegg, Mary Moore, Ida Moore Morris. Front row, left to right: Harold Hayes, Earl Moore, Lyetta Hayes, Orlo Hayes (in front), Penn Lyon, Phelps Latimer, Elystus Hayes, Carmen Moore, Ethel Moore.

Chapter 2: George Page

1 This information comes from U.S. census records in 1850, 1860, and 1870. George had a younger brother, John, who was born in 1855, and an older sister, Jane, born in 1847.

2 Margaret Henderson Floyd, *Architectural Education and Boston*. Boston: Boston Architectural Center, 1989, p. 4.

3 Floyd, p. 8–10.

4 *San Jose Daily Mercury*, January 1, 1892, p. 17.

5 *San Jose Daily Mercury*, January 1, 1892, p. 17.

6 *History of Santa Clara County*. San Francisco: Alley, Bowen & Co., 1881, p. 562. In a long biographical sketch, Hutchinson's harrowing adventures in the Gold Rush days are described, as are his later business ventures in the Alviso area and his service as justice of the peace and trustee for the town of Alviso.

   According to a lineage chart filled out in 1983 by Robert D. Page (George's grandson), his grandfather and grandmother's fathers were both born in Kennebec County, Maine.

7 Stephen Knight, *The Brotherhood*. New York: Dorset Press, 1986, p. 130.

8 John Whicher, *Masonic Beginnings in California and Hawaii*. n.p., 1931, p. 69–74.

9 Charles E. Peterson, F.A.I.A., "Pioneer Architects and Builders of Honolulu," *Hawaiian Historical Society Annual Report*, 1963, p. 7–28.

10 *California Masonry*. Los Angeles: Masonic History Company, 1936, p. 28.

11 Donlyn Lyndon, *The City Observed: Boston. A Guide to the Architecture of the Hub*. New York: Random House, 1982, p. 121.

12 *San Jose Daily Mercury*, January 1, 1892, p. 17.

13 H. S. Foote, ed. *Pen Pictures from the Garden of the World, or, Santa Clara County Illustrated*. Chicago: Lewis, 1888, p. 510.

14 Foote, p. 510. This biographical sketch of Page also states that he had been selected as the architect for the Conservatory and Chapel at the University of the Pacific, located in San Jose until the 1920s. However, an examination of records used by Robert E. Burns in writing his Ph.D. thesis, *The First Half-Century of the College of the Pacific* (Stockton: unpublished, 1946), reveals that Page did not, in fact, receive the commission. Another local architect, John Newsome was vying with Page for the commission. Newsome was apparently hired by the Board of Trustees, and Page, by the Ladies Conservatory Association. Each group was to contribute 50 percent to the building expenses.

   Notes from the Board of Trustees meeting on January 4, 1889, reveal that Newsome's plans were discussed (it is not clear if he was actually present), and then Page had an opportunity to present his plans. However, there seems to have been some concern about his plans: "Mr. Page was allowed to meet the board and give a statement of himself. He stated that he [was] employed to draw plans for, and erect, a Conservatory Building, and that if, his present plans were not satisfactory he could and would draw others, satisfactorily. Also that it would be an injury to him to be put aside, and allow some person else to take his place. Also that if the building was not erected he was to receive pay for what he had done. The plans of Mssrs. Newsome and Page were fully investigated and discussed and it was deemed advisable to adjust the matter with Mr. Page."

   Later in that same meeting, it appears that Page had won the day. "On motion it was ordered that a Committee of three be appointed, with a like Committee of Ladies to confer with Mr. Page concerning some modifications which might be made in the plans of the new Conservatory Building and that when he presented satisfactory plans, he be accepted as the architect according to the previous agreement."

   But between January 4 and the February 27, 1889, Board of Trustees meeting, something happened: "On motion it was unanimously agreed that the Acceptance of the plans drawn by Mr. Newsome, for the Conservatory of Music is conditioned upon the amount of the reliable bids not exceeding Thirty thousand dollars." Nevertheless, Newsome's road from then on was not an easy one. Bids for the brick and stone building substantially exceeded the amount available, and Newsome had to ". . . prepare plans for a building of wood, which shall not be inferior and of equal appearance and capacity to plans heretofore proposed for a building of brick and stone." The final building, which looked like stone but was made of wood, was much-photographed, appearing in every one of the college's subsequent catalogs until the campus moved to Stockton, as well as on postcards and in students' snapshot albums. The conservatory was later demolished.

Perhaps a statement of one of the participants in the January 4 meeting gives some idea of what both architects faced in this venture: "Mr. Bohl gave his opinion regarding the new building, stating that something plain and substantial, and nicely finished on the inside would be better than one with too much expense lavished on the outside."

[15] *San Jose Daily Mercury*, July 3, 1887, p. 6.

[16] Ellis A. Davis, *Davis' Commercial Encyclopedia of the Pacific Southwest*. Oakland: Ellis A. Davis, 1915, p. 401.

[17] This photograph is from Foote, p. 82.

[18] E. S. Harrison, *History of Santa Cruz County, California*. San Francisco: Pacific Press Publishing, 1892, p. 157. Harrison describes the hotel and its architect this way: "This building was designed by Mr. G. W. Page, one of San Jose's most prominent architects. The production is highly creditable to his artistic taste and common sense, being specially adapted to the elegant grounds and commanding the site which it occupies. Mr. Page is the designer of some of the finest edifices in San Jose and vicinity, particularly the magnificent villa at Eden Vale, a station on the Southern Pacific Railway a few miles south of San Jose."

However, in his book *The Sidewalk Companion to Santa Cruz Architecture* (Santa Cruz: Paper Vision Press, 1979, page 24), John Chase disputes this claim, stating that "Daniel Damkroeger was mentioned in contemporary newspaper accounts as the architect."

[19] Other architects featured in the article included Francis Reid, who wrote the article; Jacob Lenzen & Son; W. D. Van Siclen; and J. O. McKee.

[20] *San Jose Daily Mercury*, January 1, 1892, p. 17.

[21] *San Jose Daily Mercury*, January 1, 1892, p. 17.

[22] The church was originally designed for a lot on Fifth Street. When the church purchased the lot on Third Street instead, Page flipped the plan as a mirror image, with the tower on the right instead of left. He also revised the plans to remove the stone and other expensive materials he had specified for the exterior.

[23] The job list of the architectural terra cotta firm of Gladding McBean in San Francisco shows Page as the architect on two jobs during this time period, one in 1894 and the other in 1896. Unfortunately, the job list does not show the building name, but rather the name of F. A. Curtis, a San Jose masonry contractor. Curtis was later the foundation contractor for the 1905 Hayes mansion.

[24] *San Jose Mercury Herald*, May 6, 1924, p. 7.

[25] Thomas G. Thrum, *Hawaiian Annual*. Honolulu: Thomas G. Thrum, 1910.

[26] Arthur R. Andersen and Leon O. Whitsell, *California's First Century of Scottish Rite Masonry*. Oakland: n.p., 1962, p. 244.

[27] *San Jose Mercury Herald*, May 6, 1924, p. 7. Page was buried in Oak Hill Cemetery.

[28] Diane Maddex, ed. *Master Builders: A Guide to Famous American Architects*. Washington, D.C.: The Preservation Press, 1985, p. 7. Note that this book does not mention George Page.

Chapter 3: The First Hayes Mansion

[1] There are several references to the additions made to the house.

[2] By the time the family moved into the new mansion, it had more than 20 members.

3 This date is not actually specified in any document that this author has yet had access to. Rather, it is estimated from a chronology based on many different sources, including books on the Hayes family.

4 Hayes, p. 106.

5 Hayes, p. 129.

6 San Jose architect Craig Mineweaser, A.I.A., based his estimate on three full floors of space and an attic with 60 percent of the floor plan space.

7 Hayes, p. 106.

8 Hayes, p. 130.

9 Hayes, p. 129.

10 Virginia and Lee McAlester, *A Field Guide to American Houses*. New York: Knopf, 1984, p. 264.

11 *San Jose Daily Mercury*, July 31, 1899, p. 3.

12 *San Jose Daily Mercury*, July 31, 1899, p. 3.

13 Hayes, p. 186.

Chapter 4: The Second Hayes Mansion

1 Berlin, p. 12. Mrs. Berlin has, through the years, been the Hayes family descendant most interested not only in preserving the history of the mansion, but also in aiding various efforts to see it reused. Elystus was Mrs. Berlin's uncle. Her grandmother was Clara, Jay O. Hayes's wife.

2 *San Jose Daily Mercury*, August 27, 1903, p. 10.

3 When the author and Hank Lutz removed samples of the wall and floor coverings from the house before it was renovated, they found a piece of newspaper dated October 5, 1905, under the library carpet. A total of 30 samples were removed and are now in the collection of the San Jose Historical Museum.

4 *San Jose Daily Mercury*, August 27, 1905, p. 3.

5 *San Jose Daily Mercury*, July 31, 1899, p. 3.

6 The author is indebted to Virginia McAlester, coauthor with her husband Lee McAlester of *A Field Guide to American Houses*, for taking her valuable time to examine photographs and drawings of the mansion and provide her expert evaluation of its style characteristics.

7 Gladding McBean is still the premier supplier of architectural terra cotta. The firm's job lists show the Edenvale job as 1903. Most of their collection of photographs, drawings, and glass negatives are now in the California State Library (Sacramento). The collection does not, however, contain any original drawings by architects. George Page's full-page drawing, which the Gladding McBean studios interpreted and rendered in clay, is the only architect's drawing of terra cotta in the library's collection.

Chapter 5: The Hayes Estate

1 *Monterey County: Resources, History, Biography*, n.p., n.d., p. 12. According to Donald Thomas Clark (*Monterey County Place Names*, Carmel Valley, California: Kestrel Press, 1991, p. 223), the Hotel Del Monte was "the Queen of American Watering Holes." It opened in June 1880, burned down in April 1887, was rebuilt in 1888, destroyed again by fire in September 1924, rebuilt and reopened once more in 1926. In 1942, it was taken over by the Navy as a preflight school. It is now the home of the United States Naval Postgraduate School.

2 These photographs were taken by Andrew P. Hill. His name is stamped on the back with his address listed as "The Doughtery Building." This building was demolished in the April 1906 earthquake so the photographs must have been taken before then. Hill was a painter and photographer whose photographs of the redwoods in the Santa Cruz mountains earlier in this century led to the creation of the Big Basin Redwoods State Park. Because of the quality of light in the original photographs, the author suspects that Hill also photographed the

inside of the Hayes mansion (see Chapter 4). Since the family did not completely move into the mansion until just before Thanksgiving 1905, one can conclude that the photographs were taken between that time and April 1906.

[3] *San Jose Daily Mercury*, July 31, 1899, p. 3.

[4] Foote, p. 254. Although there is no information to corroborate her theory, the author suspects that an architect (perhaps George Page) was hired to design the carriage barn, simply because it was so elegant.

[5] *San Jose Daily Mercury*, January 12, 1894, p. 6.

[6] *San Jose Daily Mercury*, January 1, 1892, p. 17.

Chapter 6: The Gem is Polished

[1] The San Jose City Council functions as the board of directors for the Redevelopment Agency.

[2] Author's conversation with Jeff Davenport on January 18, 1994.

[3] Author's conversation with Dennis Meidinger on March 7, 1994.

[4] Author's conversation with Judy Stabile on February 16, 1994.

Acknowledgments

Architectural consultation by Craig Mineweaser, A.I.A., John Frolli, and Guy Rothwell of Mineweaser & Associates, Architects, San Jose, California.

Thanks to: Clare Berlin; Bishop Museum (Honolulu, Hawaii); Anne Bloomfield; Boston Public Library; Bostonian Society; Lilyann Brannon; California State Archives; Prof. A. J. Chewning, Department of Design, Art, Architecture and Planning, University of Cincinnati; Laura Condon, Society for the Preservation of New England Antiquities; Jeff Davenport, Renaissance Conference Company; Maurice Dunbar, De Anza College; Minxie Fannin, Society for Architectural History, New England Chapter; Janene Ford, Holt-Atherton Department of Special Collections, University of the Pacific Libraries; John Gonzales, California State Library; Joanne Grant, *San Jose Mercury News*; April Halberstadt; Hans Halberstadt; Hawaii Historical Society; Hawaii State Archives; Hawaii State Library; Judi Henderson; Scott Hinrichs; Virginia Huffman; Iolani Palace; John Kinset, California Room, Martin Luther King Main Library, San Jose; Nelle Kopacz, Iron County Historical Society; Gary Kurutz, California State Library; Glory Anne Laffey, Sourisseau Academy for State and Local History, San Jose State University; Waverly B. Lowell, National Archives—Pacific Sierra Region; Hank Lutz; Deputy San Jose City Manager Dan McFadden; Virginia McAlester; Leslie Masunaga, San Jose Historical Museum; Ray Maurin, Ironwood Area Historical Society; Dennis Meidinger, A.I.A.; Richard Newlin; Robert Douglas Page; Joan Pedersen; John Pelton; Punahou School, Honolulu, Hawaii; Kimberly Shilland, MIT Museum; Judy Stabile; Special Collections, University Library, University of California, Santa Cruz; Nancy Valby, San Jose Historical Museum; Don Walker, Holt-Atherton Department of Special Collections, University of the Pacific Libraries; John Wrenn, AIA Archives; and to everyone else who offered advice, enthusiasm, information, and support.

Permissions

The author expresses her gratitude for permission to reprint the following copyrighted material:

Various excerpts from the *San Jose Daily Mercury* and *The Spirit Dominant* by Louisa Johnson Clay, Mercury Herald Company, n.d. Used by permission of the *San Jose Mercury News*.

One quotation from the *San Francisco Examiner*. Used by permission of the *San Francisco Examiner*.

One quotation from *Architectural Education in Boston* by Margaret Henderson Floyd. Copyright 1989 by Margaret Henderson Floyd. Used by permission of Margaret Henderson Floyd.

One quotation from *Master Builders: A Guide to Famous American Architects* edited by Diane Maddex. Copyright 1985 by the Preservation Press. Used by permission of the National Trust for Historic Preservation.

Quotations from *The Hayes Family: Reminiscences of Elystus L. Hayes* by Clare Berlin. Copyright 1971 by Clare Berlin. Used by permission of Clare Berlin.

Quotations from *Mary Hayes Chynoweth: A Spiritual Life* by Clara Lyon Hayes. Copyright 1964 by Clare Berlin. Used by permission of Clare Berlin.

One quotation from *The Brotherhood* by Stephen Knight. Copyright 1986 by Stephen Knight. Used by permission of Dorset Press.

Index

Note that page numbers in italics refer to photographs.

About the Author

The Gem of Edenvale was Nancy Newlin's "dream project." With a lifelong interest in historical architecture and preservation, she first encountered the Hayes mansion in 1989. Two years later, after she had an opportunity to go inside the mansion, she knew that she wanted to tell its story—not just the story of the building itself, but the story of the people who built it, the people who lived in it, and the people who saved it from destruction.

During the yearlong process of converting the Hayes Mansion into the Hayes Renaissance Conference Center, Ms. Newlin was on site, collecting samples of original materials for preservation and witnessing the demolition and reconstruction first hand. She took over 500 photographs to document the process. Some of those photographs appear in this book.

Ms. Newlin has years of experience in research and writing. She has served on the board of directors of the Preservation Action Council of San Jose and was editor of its newsletter. She holds a bachelor's degree in graphic design and a master's degree in library science. This is her first book on historical architecture.